OAK LEAVES AND LAVENDER

BOOKS BY SEAN O'CASEY

Plays

Two Plays
Juno and the Paycock
The Plough and the Stars
Five Irish Plays
The Star Turns Red
Purple Dust
Red Roses for Me

Biography

I Knock at the Door
Pictures in the Hallway
Drums Under the Windows

OAK LEAVES
AND LAVENDER

OR

A WARLD ON WALLPAPER

BY

SEAN O'CASEY

LONDON
MACMILLAN & CO. LTD
1946

COPYRIGHT

TO

LITTLE JOHNNY GRAYBURN

WHO, IN HIS SAILOR SUIT, PLAYED FOOTBALL
WITH ME ON A CHALFONT LAWN
AND AFTERWARDS GALLANTLY FELL
IN THE BATTLE OF ARNHEM

CHARACTERS IN ORDER OF APPEARANCE

PRELUDE OF THE SHADOWS

1ST LADY DANCER
1ST GENTLEMAN DANCER
2ND LADY DANCER
2ND GENTLEMAN DANCER
YOUNG SON OF TIME
3RD LADY DANCER
3RD GENTLEMAN DANCER

THE PLAY

FEELIM O'MORRIGUN, *Butler to Dame Hatherleigh*
MONICA PENRHYN, *Abraham Penrhyn's daughter*
MARK, *a Home Guard*
JENNIE }
JOY } *Land Girls*
1ST SPECIAL CONSTABLE SILLERY
2ND SPECIAL CONSTABLE DILLERY
DRISHOGUE, *Feelim's son in the Air Force*
EDGAR, *the Dame's son in the Air Force*
MRS. WATCHIT, *the Dame's Housekeeper*
DAME HATHERLEIGH, *Dame of a manor-house in the West*
MICHAEL, *a Home Guard*
MRS. DEEDA TUTTING, *a Visitor*
3RD HOME GUARD
ABRAHAM PENRHYN, *a Small Farmer*
MR. CONSTANT, *a Resident eager to get his wife to America*
A MAN, *Leader of Deputation demanding shelters*
POBJOY, *a Conscientious Objector*
AN OLD WOMAN OF SEVENTY
FOREMAN IN FACTORY
FELICITY, *a Land Girl*
A SELLER OF LAVENDER

SCENES

THE PRELUDE.—The great room of a Manorial House
of a long-past century, when the lights are low, and
the flickering shadows softly come and go.
ACT I.—The same, when the lights go up.
ACT II.—The same.
ACT III.—The same.

———————

TIME.—During the Battle of Britain.

PRELUDE

SCENE : *The room before us shows something like what a central room in a Manorial House of the Long Ago might have been, had we been there to see it. It is gorgeous, but has, architecturally, a chaste and pleasing beauty. Its broad and beaded panelling runs across the walls in simple lines and ovals, so that a dreamy engineer might see in them the rods and motionless shafts of machinery. Two high-up circular pieces of panelling, one on each side of the back wall, have whorling edges on them so that the same engineer might fancy them into germs of revolving cog-wheels. Three great chandeliers, at regular intervals, droop from the ceiling, and the dreamy engineer could see in them the possible beginnings of gigantic gantries. The three semicircular windows at back, the centre much larger than those at either side, might become, in the far-away future, the head of a great machine, everlastingly turning out fantastic weapons of war. The big bureau might turn into a fine lathe turning out finely-formed tools. The columns round a wide doorway, on the right corner towards the back, might evolve into great ponderous hammers pounding shapes into hard and burnished steel. The wide floor-place below these columns might turn*

I

into a mighty coke oven to smelt the steel for the hammers. The end of a grand piano, sticking out on the right — for part only of the great room is visible — might be the beginning of a monster table for the drawing of blue-prints, the skeletons of those things for which the steel melts and the hammers fall. To the side of the window on the right of the back wall, between it and the doorway, stands a tall gold-framed clock that might in the future become a delicate wheel, turning the others, and setting the machinery going with zest and resolution. Above the clock is a circular glass bulb, shaped like the disk of a plain and simple monstrance. All this is hardly seen when the play begins, for the light playing on them seems to come from the ghosts of many candles.

Three couples, dressed mistily in the garb of the eighteenth century, come in dancing, forming a triangle of figures ; they dance to a minuet, the notes played on a piano, a little slowly, and perhaps a little stiffly. The dancers move slowly and stiffly with the melody ; indeed, they dance as if they found it hard to move, and did so as if in a dream ; or as if their thoughts were on things almost forgotten, rather than on the dance. The wide-flowing skirts and high-powdered hair of the ladies are dimly grey like the twilight around them, their shapes picked out by narrow lines of black round the flounces and narrower lines *following the margins of the bodices. The broad-skirted coats of the men and their wigs are of the same dim colour with lapels and cuffs faintly shown by similar narrow lines of black braid, while from each hip sticks out a shadow of a sword, slender as a needle, but black like the braid. The music, while faint and low and stiff, strikes a slightly deeper note whenever the couples courtesy to each other.*

When the first couple reaches that part of the room close to, and directly in front of, the central window, they all halt and stand motionless, the music becoming even fainter than it had been before. When they speak, they do so in seemingly level tones, scarcely giving any inflexion to, or putting any emphasis on, their words. Their voices, too, are low, a pitch or two above a whisper ; but clearly heard.

Beside the clock, leaning carelessly but grace- fully against it, is YOUNG SON OF TIME, *a young, handsome lad of twenty or twenty-one. He is dressed in a close-fitting suit of vivid emerald green, imagination might think sym- bolical of youth's earnest and warm vigour ; from his shoulders hangs a deep sable cloak which imagination might think indicative of the threat of old age bound to come, sooner or later ; and on his head is a conical hat of gleaming silver which imagination again might think symbolic of the remembrance of things past. His voice — when he speaks —*

3

*is clear and bell-like, and there is a note of
authority and finality in what he says.*

IST LADY DANCER
(*with a sigh*)
I'm tired ; I shouldn't be, but I am.

IST GENTLEMAN DANCER
(*with a sigh*)
So am I ; but we must go on, and hold our own
among the shadows.

IST LADY DANCER
I'm cold, too, and I can't see too well. Is the
light getting dim ?

IST GENTLEMAN DANCER
Most of the candles give light no longer — look !
their golden glow is gone.

IST LADY DANCER
(*echoing*)
Light no longer. Golden glow is gone. Look !
Oh no ; I'm afraid to look. Do not see ; do not
hear. Let us move behind.
[*They all dance slow and stiff again till the
first couple is away from the window, and
the second couple takes its place. Then the
dance stops, though the music, barely heard,
still goes on slow and stiff, too.*

2ND LADY DANCER
I am full of loneliness, Nigel. As we came in no

crowds pressed against the watchmen and the link-
boys to stare at us. The street was empty, and
no flame came from the torches the link-boys held,
though further on the street was full of sound.

2ND GENTLEMAN DANCER

We need no flame from torches now.

2ND LADY DANCER

But why do our torches burn no longer ?

2ND GENTLEMAN DANCER

Burning torches now are in the hands of others.

2ND LADY DANCER

Hands of others ?   Whose hands, Nigel ?

2ND GENTLEMAN DANCER

The hands of the dull and hangdog crowd.

YOUNG SON OF TIME
(the clock ticks loudly)

Time has put them into the itching hand of the
people.

2ND LADY DANCER

I'm afraid, Nigel — the guillotine.

2ND GENTLEMAN DANCER

Be at peace, sweet lady : the crowd can never
come here ; they cannot harm us now.

2ND LADY DANCER

Hold me closer, Nigel, and let us go.   Oh, try to
hold me closer.

5

[*He takes no notice of what she says, as if he
    had not heard.*

YOUNG SON OF TIME
(*clock ticks loudly*)

Go ; the clock will never strike again for you.
Go, and leave the fair deeds you did to stir faint
thoughts of grandeur in fond memory's mind.
    [*These two dancers move away to the stiff tune
        of the faint music, to give place to the third
        couple who dance towards the window till
        they reach its centre.
    From the street, outside, is heard the tender,
        musical, and low voice of a girl offering
        lavender for sale in a chant of praise.*

GIRL
(*singing*)

Won't you buy my bonnie lavender,
Tender-scented, tiny flower ;
Giving honied gardens to the bees,
Fresh'ning ev'ry passing hour.
    Lavender, lavender,
Won't you buy my bonnie laven-lavender !

3RD LADY DANCER
(*in a voice faintly frightened*)

What voice is that ? Something strange touches
me from another world. What is it ? Where was
it ? Oh, Ned, the deep silences of where we
always are force a cry from me that can never
come ; and I am frightened. Some sound is

6

hurting me. It is so sad no sign is left to show the strength we had, or the grace and elegance that led it forward.

3RD GENTLEMAN DANCER

The world shall never lose what the world has ever given.

3RD LADY DANCER

Not a single torchlight in the street ; not a glow from a single window ; not a solitary gleam from a welcoming doorway. When we were there, the place was gay with torch and candle. Oh, Ned, it is very dark !

3RD GENTLEMAN DANCER

It is dark to us ; but Goldsmith, Berkeley, Boyle, Addison, Hone, Swift, and Sheridan still bear flaming torches through the streets of life.

3RD LADY DANCER

But the common crew can never see the flame. (*A slow red glare appears in the sky ; a point of deep red in the distance, thinning to a mauvish-red gleam as it shines through the window, touching, with a wan warmth, the dim grey costumes of the dancers. With a faint start.*)   I feel the colour change ! What is it ? And afar is anxiety and woe. What sends this sense of danger to us ?

3RD GENTLEMAN DANCER

It comes from those who came from us, for England is at war.

7

No, no, not war ; the flame of war could never light up London.

> [*The two other couples come closer to the window, though the three couples stand still in a triangle, the apex formed by the third couple at centre of window.*

Look ! The buildings topple like the town of Troy. The flames get wider. The enemy is striking home to England's inmost heart.

Oh, let's go on dancing, and never look again.

Look ! There, in the midst of the red foliage, the dome of St. Paul's stands out like a black and withering lotus blossom !

Oh, Maurice, is England and the world to lose the glow from a thousand tapers, the colour-shining vestments of the bishops, the jewels in altar and gems in cross, the chorus of sacred song, and the blessed peace of public absolution !

And the gay jest from careless lips of gallants on the pompous steps outside.

2ND GENTLEMAN DANCER
(*stiffly putting right hand to his left hip*)
Where are our swords ?

3RD AND 1ST GENTLEMEN DANCERS
(*echoing him*)
Where are our swords ?

YOUNG SON OF TIME
They lie resting, rusting deep where no man
wanders now.

2ND GENTLEMAN DANCER
Where is Marlborough and where is Clive ?

3RD GENTLEMAN DANCER
Where is Wolfe and where is Wellesley ?

YOUNG SON OF TIME
England's orphan'd of her greatest men.   She is
alone at last, and she is lost.

1ST GENTLEMAN DANCER
The shadows will go forth to fight for England.

LADY DANCERS
(*together*)
But where are your swords ?   (*Sadly*) All that's
left us is a fainting memory of love.

YOUNG SON OF TIME
Time has brought a change.   The silken things
that sheltered rosy bodies are in rags ; the rubies,

flushing shy on milky bosoms, have gone to dust ;
and the needle-pointed swords, all hemmed with
jewels, that a common man might deem it joy to
die on, are blunt and leaden-bladed now.

1ST LADY DANCER

Let us dance, let us dance, and never seek a
glance at anything.

2ND LADY DANCER

Let us dance, and try to glide to things remembered.

3RD LADY DANCER

Let us dance, always near, but never close together.

> [*They resume the slow dance of the minuet,
> and gradually pass out of sight. As they
> dance, the voice of the* LAVENDER SELLER *is
> heard again, chanting her wares, her song
> ending just as the dancers fade from view.*

LAVENDER SELLER

(*singing in a low, rather sad voice*)
Won't you buy my bonnie lavender,
Ladies, for your fine chemises ?
Its fragrance rare will make them finer still,
Tempting close the hand that pleases.
Lavender, lavender,
Won't you buy my bonnie laven-lavender !

END OF PRELUDE

ACT I

*The dancers are no longer there ; and mild lights,
that have been shaded slightly to reduce the
power of their glow, show us the room plainly.
It is as it was when the shades were dancing,
though the panelling seems a little stylised
away from its normal lines and curving.*
FEELIM O'MORRIGUN *and* MONICA PENRHYN
*are busy handling stuff to make a blackout for
the window on the left, the central window
and the smaller one to the right having been
already covered to their satisfaction.*
FEELIM *is a man of forty-five years, wiry, slender,
and as cunning as a fox (except when he is in a
temper), which he somewhat resembles with
his thin protruding nose and reddish hair,
now tinged, though very slightly, with grey.
He is dressed from the waist up as a second-
hand butler might be, creased black swallow-
tail coat, black waistcoat, white shirt, and
black tie, the bow askew ; below these he
wears the trousers and leggings of a Home
Guard.* MONICA *is a young lass, sweet and
twenty ; pretty face, well-made body, bright
eyes, a little pensive at times. A girl who
would be able to concentrate on what was
actually before her to do. She is dressed in a
neat brown skirt and a bodice of a warmer
brown. All are partially concealed by a rough*

unbleached apron. A gaily-coloured scarf covers her brown hair, and round her arm is a white band with a tiny red cross in its centre.

MONICA

I wish you were my dad, instead of my own. I've borne with him since I was ten, when my mother, too tired to go on, left the pair of us to make the worst of it.

FEELIM

Strange, isn't it? I miss my own old girl far more than Drishogue misses his mother. Odd man, your old man. His conscience is a menace to most people. I never could understand men interested in religion.

MONICA

We better stir ourselves.

FEELIM

It wants near a half-hour to blackout yet. How's Mary?

MONICA

Going on fine, though she won't be able to do much for a while.

FEELIM

Fool! Putting a blackout up in th' dark, an' steppin' from th' window-sill on to a chair that wasn't there! An' how's Tom?

MONICA

Going on fine, though his hand won't let him do much for a week or so.

FEELIM

(*venomously*)

Another fool! Not able to drive a nail into wood without shoving his hand through a window and cutting a vein open! Th' house'll be an hospital before this blackout's finished. (*Something tumbling is heard outside, followed by the crash of breaking glass. With venomous resignation*) Oh! There's another casualty now!

[MARK, *of the Home Guard, rushes frantically in through the door faced by the columns. He is in rough civilian dress, wears a khaki forage cap, and has a wide khaki armlet with the words "Home Guard" on it in black. A tall, well-knit man of twenty-seven.*

MARK

(*excitedly*)

Miss Monica, quick, come! One of the men cloakin' a window, top of chair, top of another, top of a table, 'as pitched down, lookin' like 'ee's broken back, or somethin'!

FEELIM

(*clicking his tongue in exasperated disgust as* MONICA *runs out with* MARK)

Dtch dtch dtch! The foe'll do less injury to us than we're doin' to ourselves!

[*Two Land Girls come in by the door with the columns. One is named* JENNIE *and the other* JOY. JENNIE *is a sturdy lass, inclined to be slightly florid, and though she is*

13

*fairly well educated as things go, having
had a secondary schooling, she is at times
somewhat rough and strident in her manner.
She is enticingly shaped, even a little
voluptuous-looking. She has a head of
thick, dark, honey-yellow hair which she
often tosses aside when she feels it cluster-
ing on her forehead. She is twenty-four,
full of confidence, and likes to be thought
a little Rabelaisian. Her companion is
plainer, not so confident, ready to follow
JENNIE and look up to her. Her brown hair
is straighter, but is at present in the grip of
a permanent wave. She is slimmer, and,
though she enjoys any coarse sally from
JENNIE, she tries, at times, to appear to be
very refined. She has had to be satisfied with
an ordinary Council School upbringing, but
she is a country lass, and no fool. Both
wear brown breeches, high rubber boots,
brown smocks, with coloured kerchiefs,
fixed peasant-wise, around their heads.*

JENNIE
(*weariedly*)

Oh, God, I'm tired! Every bone and nerve in
me is aching.

JOY

So's mine. Suppose we'll get used to it in time.

JENNIE

Long time, dear. (*To* FEELIM) Give two worn-out
girls a spot of gin an' apple-juice, will you?

14

FEELIM

(going to bureau to get the drinks)

An' then go up to have rest, an' get outa th' way
here where people have to work !

JENNIE

(scornfully)

You don't know what work is. You should work
among cows. (*To* JOY) You'd want to be born
with animals like cows, dear. Study their likes
and dislikes, says the farmer. If you do, he says,
you'll get better results from the feedin' you give
them. D'ja know what he told me ? The highly-
strung cow always makes a good milker. J'ever
know the like ! Film stars aren't in it with cows.
Thank God I'm off the job with cows. Too
temperamental for me, my dear. I'm not sure
yet whether a thousand-gallon cow's one giving a
thousand gallons a year, or a thousand a week !
No, I said, take me off cows, and put me on the
hay.

JOY

We saved the hay anyhow.

JENNIE

We did ; but that'll be forgot, while the failure
with cows will live after us.

JOY

Let it, dear.

JENNIE

Hear, hear ! (*To* FEELIM, *who hands her a drink*)

Thanks. (*As she stands near window, she sniffs gently.*) What scent is that now stealing in through the window?

JOY

I don't smell anything. Scent of hay from the ricks, maybe.

JENNIE
(*sniffing again*)

No, not hay, old or new. Lavender — that's what it is — lavender! Must be a bed of it somewhere. If mother knew what's going on, now, she'd have a fit! When there's a war on, you can't turn a hot day of it into a holy or a silent night.

JOY

Hard, dear; but us must do our best.

JENNIE

When a girl's beneath trees with a moon flitting in and out of the branches, there's sure to be someone singing a bar of love's old sweet song somewhere handy. (*To* FEELIM) What d'ye think, old emerald isle?

FEELIM
(*coldly*)

I'm not listening, thank you.

JENNIE
(*mockingly*)

Aha, my boy, I've seen your roving eye often

trying to glimpse what was under the green jersey. Well, I don't blame you. (*She drinks.*) It's hard when hand can't follow the eye to start the first few notes of love's fiddle fantasia. (*She sings :*)

When we stretch'd ourselves down in a hurry,
Beneath th' soft shade of a tree,
Th' moon threw her mantle of silver
O'er red-headed Johnny and me.

Stars twinkled a welcome, and wonder'd
How we far'd under Cynthia's shawl ;
No girl ever suffer'd such pleasure,
Since Adam gave Eve her first fall !

Ho, then, for young man and for maiden —
Fair jewels of love fiercely aglow —
Who save life eternal from fadin',
An' keep a tir'd world on th' go !

FEELIM
(*disgusted*)

Dtch dtch !

JOY
(*pretending to be shocked — but unable to stop a giggle*)

Jennie, you're terrible !

JENNIE

Shakespeare, my dear.

JOY
(*astonished*)

Is it ? Us always thought he was a highbrow.

JENNIE

Seems he went over the shallow end sometimes.

JOY

Where does that saucy bit occur ? Us 'ud love
t'read it.

JENNIE

Ask me another ! Let's go an' have a rest — we
have to meet the boys later on, y'know.

FEELIM

(*to* JENNIE *as the girls are going out*)
I wouldn't be messin' round after Mr. Edgar —
his mother doesn't like it.

JENNIE

(*savagely — as she goes out*)
She can lump it !
  [*With an expression of hurt disappointment
  on his face,* FEELIM *goes back to his work
  with the blackout as* MONICA *returns to help
  him.*

FEELIM

Well ?

MONICA

Nothing much ; little shock and sprained arm —
that's all.

FEELIM

God help me, but wasn't I a fool to come here
at all !

MONICA

Is the thought of the bombing getting you down ?

18

FEELIM

Bombing! Not the bombing — the people. Bombing'll never frighten me.

MONICA

There's nothing to be ashamed of in a little fear. I've gone through a little of it, so I know.

FEELIM

It's the people — not able to do anything without breakin' back, arm, leg, or something. Oh, amn't I sorry I came!

MONICA

Why did you come, then?

FEELIM

If I knew why, one of th' world's mysteries would be solved.

MONICA

But you must have had a reason for coming?

FEELIM

Of course I had — I wanted a job, and the owner here wanted a capable man, so the two extremes met. There's not much to choose from in Knocknawhishogue. I happened across an English paper advertising for a butler in a house of six servants; so, fearing there wasn't too much to be done, I replied, sayin' I was fully qualified, though all my credentials went down in a torpedoed ship.

MONICA

(*interested*)

You have been through something, then; I'd
never have guessed it.

FEELIM

I felt it worse than me friend who told me about
it, for he was all right afther a week of hot
blankets an' brandy; but I'm not quite th'
betther of it yet.

MONICA

(*astonished and doubtful*)

You weren't, yourself, flung into the sea, then?

FEELIM

(*astonished*)

Me? No, not actually, for I wasn't in th' ship.

MONICA

(*disillusioned*)

Then how the hell could you be as bad as the
poor man sodden to the soul in sea-water!

FEELIM

(*resentful*)

Amn't I afther tellin' you, I was worse than him!
Have you no imagination, girl? Hadn't he th'
elation of comin' safe out of it all, while I'm stuck
strugglin' in it still?

MONICA

(*mystified*)

Stuck struggling in what?

FEELIM
(*irritated at her want of understanding*)
Aw, th' wather, woman !

MONICA
(*dubiously*)
I see.

FEELIM
Near time you did. Well, we better get this up.
(*He goes to the window with blackout.*) Hope it'll
fit. (*He cocks his nose into the air, and sniffs.*)
What's that I smell, now ? (*He sniffs again.*)
Lavender. It's here, too ; seems to be all over
the house.

MONICA
(*suddenly and with roughness*)
Oh, shut up, man ! It's not lavender you smell.
And if it be, keep it to yourself, keep it to yourself !

FEELIM
(*astounded*)
What's gone wrong with you, girl ?

MONICA
I don't believe it, I don't !

FEELIM
(*a little frightened — going closer to her*)
Don't believe what, woman ?

MONICA
The old wife's tale that whenever death is near,

21

the scent of lavender spreads over the house, and shadows of men in knee-breeches and wigs, with women in out-fanning skirts, dance silently in the bigger rooms of the manor. Dame Hatherleigh's as full of it as she is of her British Israel and the lost Ten Tribes.

FEELIM
(*startled*)
Here ? Do these ghostly dancers assemble here ?

MONICA
Here ; I tell you, I've never seen them ; never !

FEELIM
(*awestruck*)
Is it tellin' me th' house is haunted y'are ?

MONICA
(*shaking his arm*)
It's superstition, man. Don't believe it.

FEELIM
(*in anguished tones*)
Oh, I guessed there was a snag in it ! Come over at once, says Colonel Hatherleigh in his letter to me ; an' quite jovial about it, too. Come along, old boy, says he ; almost anyone'll do me now. You'll do fine, says he, if you can do anything, for the place is destitute since my poor man died so unexpectedly. (*Catching* MONICA's *arm excitedly*) How did th' man die ?

22

MONICA

Blast from a bomb blew the poor man over the highest barn in the county.

FEELIM

(*angrily*)

An' why wasn't I informed of all this ? Oh, what an innocent, poor gobeen I am, too, to be coaxed into this thrap ! An' I insistin' me son should come, too, without an inklin' that he was itchin' to get into th' Air Force, where he is now. Uncivilised duplicity everywhere ! An' while Colonel Hatherleigh hied himself off to th' ease an' comfort of th' front, here I'm sthranded with his wife, an' women set to talk me into a wild dilerium ! An' all for a job in a house haunted by night, an' a bedlam by day with workers on th' new aerodrome, Home Guard units, air-raid wardens, first-aid post, Land Girl hostel, an' rest camp for th' bombed-out an' evacuees ; with me in th' centre an' on th' fringe to keep harmony an' ordher !

MONICA

(*impatiently*)

For God's sake, let's forget about this old wife's fable !

FEELIM

How ?

MONICA

By working to get the blackout up.

FEELIM

It's gettin' too dark to see proper. I'll switch th'

23

light on — a second won't matther. Dim twilight makes me feel a trifle queer. (*He sets down switch, and a bright light glows among the chandeliers.*) That's bether.

IST CONSTABLE
(*outside — with a roar*)

Put out that light !

FEELIM
(*as he runs and turns up the switch again*)

God Almighty, there's a constable behind every bush here !

MONICA

We'll manage all right ; hand it to me when I get on the ladder.

> [*She mounts the ladder, and* FEELIM *hands her the blackout to be put in its place.*

FEELIM
(*suddenly going tense*)

What's that ? Is that a rustle o' skirts behind me !

> [DILLERY, *a constable, appears behind them, and shines a torch to where they work.*

DILLERY

You can't be puttin' on lights sudden-like ! I suppose you know it's an offence to show an unobscured light ? Us'll 'ave to report if it happens again. An' window above 'as a seam of light showin' left side. Better settle she at once. Suppose you know seam can be seen five miles up sky ? Us 'as given a last warnin', mind !

> [*He goes out again.*

24

FEELIM

Fuss an' fury. God must ha' had a rare laugh
when He made a serious Englishman.

MONICA

(*bending down from ladder towards* FEELIM —
tensely)

You didn't really hear it, did you ?

FEELIM

Hear what, hear what, girl ?

MONICA

The seductive rustle of the skirts ?

FEELIM

(*upset again*)

Yes ! No ! No, no ! Why d'ye keep puttin' it
in me mind ? (MONICA *is silent.*) Why, why
d'j'ask me, I'm sayin' ?

MONICA

Only to sense the perfume isn't so bad as to see
or feel the dancers.

FEELIM

(*very frightened*)

I'm sure I saw them ! Pale figures whirlin' about
in gay-coloured skirts — their flounces touched
me face !

MONICA

You didn't see, you couldn't have seen them !

They don't have bright colours: grey and shadowy they all are. Like young Sir Nigel.

FEELIM

What Sir Nigel, which Sir Nigel, whose Sir Nigel?

MONICA

Him whose picture's in the corner there: who kissed his bride, and spurred away to fall on the field of Blenheim. Less'n a year after, they saw her rise to dance with a young gallant in grey, swooning when the grey shadow faded out of her arms, to die an hour after, murmuring that eternity would open and end for her dancing in the arms of Nigel; in this room; in this very room.

FEELIM

(*awestruck*)

In this very room! (*He crosses himself.*) Jesus, Mary, an' Joseph between us an' all harm!

> [*They remain silent and still for a few moments; then* FEELIM, *to conceal his fear, gets angry.*

FEELIM

(*angrily*)

Why do you keep harpin' on these childish rumours, girl? You'll be gettin' yourself down if you go on. What's it to us how a damsel died two hundhred year ago?

MONICA

She's still a symbol of a thousand girls kissing a

26

lover farewell, while chafing death, at his elbow, waits to guide him safely to the battlefield.

Ever since you came into the room you've been screeching about death ! It's gettin' a bit monotonous. If what you say's thrue, a house like this shouldn't be left standin'. Thry to be a little livelier, a young one like you. (*As she slowly raises the blackout to cover the window*) Oh, fix it, fix it, till we get a comfortable light in the place ! (*She hangs it up. The moment it's fixed, he rushes over, and switches on the light.*) There's a wee slit of light to the left ; hammer a nail in to keep th' cloth close. (*He hands her hammer and nail. Some moments before, the faint tramp of marching men is heard, becoming louder, till it sounds close to the window.*) Th' Home Guard pit-pattin' about again ! Old men manœuverin' themselves into an early grave. I wonder Dame Hatherleigh lets them make a playground of her grounds. (*Up to* MONICA) Go on — why don't you nail it ?

My hand's trembling !

                    (*irritated*)

What's it thremblin' for ? If you go on, I'll soon be as bad as y'are yourself. Get down, and I'll do it.

　　　[*The tramp of regular marching feet is heard*

*loudly now, accompanied by orders shouted
by the leader of the company, as* MONICA
comes down the ladder, and FEELIM *goes up.
The leader's commands are given in sten-
torian tones, the first word being slightly
drawn out, the second delivered in a roar.*

HOME GUARD LEADER
(*outside*)

R-i-g-h-t wheel ! (*More quietly*) In the line, in
the line. Left, left. (*A roar*) A-b-o-u-t turn !
(*Short, sharp tone*) Left, left, left. (*Quietly*)
In the file, in the file.

FEELIM
(*clicking his tongue in scorn*)

Dtch dtch ! It's pathetic. They think they're
marchin' through Georgia.

LEADER
(*in an extra loud order*)

L-e-f-t wheel !
[*There is a crash of breaking glass.* FEELIM
*slips quickly down the ladder as the spear-
head of a pike shoots through the window
he is covering.*

FEELIM
(*soberly, but in anger*)

See that ? They won't leave a single thing whole
in the place before they're done. It's only by
God's mercy that I wasn't impaled !

28

(*outside — shouting*)

Put out that light!

FEELIM

(*running over to the switch to do so — in anguish*)
Ooh! There's the eye that never sleeps again.
(*To* MONICA) Shove the blackout into its place,
and we'll do something to the broken pane tomorrow. God only knows what damage would
be done were these fellas armed with slings and
smooth pebbles from a runnin' brook. Danger
from within' an' danger from without. (*He
switches on the light again.*) Now we can see
through the silly, sombre fantasies of the darkness.

MONICA
(*seriously*)

I hear Drishogue and Edgar coming — I
shouldn't say anything about the dancers. No
use of letting sad thoughts invade the quiet live-
liness of their outlook.

FEELIM

Is it me mention it? Even if I did, Drishogue
wouldn't believe a word of it, no more'n meself.
And I've something else to think of beyond
shadows — where's me schedule? (*He searches
on the table.*) Here it is. (*He runs a finger through
the leaves of an exercise-book and reads from it.*)
" Stirrup-pump class; Fire-drill exercise; Gas-
mask practice; Discussion on Hens most suitable
for people and disthrict; Red Cross meeting;

Dig for Victory Committee "; no end to them. (*To* MONICA) Monica, darling, for all we know, sinisther persons may be playin' thricks about the house, an' it might be well to put a Home Guard man on duty at nights.

MONICA

(*warningly*)

Sshush !

> [DRISHOGUE *and* EDGAR *come in slowly, looking rather bored. When* DRISHOGUE *sees* MONICA *his face brightens into a wide smile. He is a tall lad of twenty or so ; a thoughtful, tense face, which is somewhat mocked at by a turned-up, freckled nose.* EDGAR, *nearly as tall, is of the same age ; his face is plump where* DRISHOGUE'S *is lean ; careless good nature, and, perhaps, less imagination, tends to make it, maybe, a trifle too placid. The two young men wear the uniform of Air Force Cadets.*

DRISHOGUE

(*sighing with boredom*)

Well, we'll know soon ; as for me, I know I've passed the tests. Oh, how I long to take the sky by storm ! (*Going over to* MONICA — *eagerly*) Monica, dear, are you going to work all night ? I thought you'd be ready to come out an'hour ago.

MONICA

I won't be long now ; I'll run off and change.

30

EDGAR

If you see Jennie, tell her I'm waiting here.

MONICA

I'll tell her ; she's resting ; we'll probably come down together.   [*She goes out.*

EDGAR
(*to* DRISHOGUE)

A bonny lass, boy ; and a brave one, too.

FEELIM

Sensible and sound enough, if her mind wasn't adorned with a lot of nonsense.

DRISHOGUE

Nonsense ?   What nonsense ?

FEELIM
(*carelessly*)

Oh, a restless readiness to believe that the deeply dead, who once lived here, can come again to counterfeit in shadow the life they lived before ; and men as shrewd as we can hear the silent stir of their ghostly dancing.

[*There are a few moments of silence as* DRISHOGUE *and* EDGAR *look at each other.*

DRISHOGUE
(*to* EDGAR)

There, I told you !   I'd swear I heard last night the timid music of a frightened minuet.

31

EDGAR

(*with good-natured mockery*)

Newcomers always hear strange things in an old house, Drishogue. They expect them, and they come ; a Londoner here, recently, swore he saw shadows in his room peggin' away in the Lambeth Walk. If Feelim sees them, he's sure to see them doing an Irish jig. Let's be sensible : the past is gone for ever, and can never have any influence upon us. A new life, broken from everything gone before, will shortly be before us.

DRISHOGUE

No, Edgar, you're wrong : the past has woven us into what we are. (*With a yawn.*) How I wish the fight to come closer ! This coloured idleness is killing me.

EDGAR

Take care ; you may get your wish. This idleness is giving us a longer life. Eight weeks — the average life of an airman : not long enough for me. I don't want to come toppling down in the drink. I can endure many more evenings with Jennie.

DRISHOGUE

Don't you ever get tired of walking or lying with Jennie ?

EDGAR

Often ; but with her the tiredness is always restful. She's grand for the time being.

32

But you don't value her enough to want to spend a lifetime with her ?

EDGAR

Well, hardly ; in the cool of the evening, in the deep dusk of the night, she is lovely ; but I shouldn't care to have to welcome her the first thing in the morning.

FEELIM

A woman's a blessing when th' sun's setting, but a burden when she's rising.   But don't talk too loud, boys — I've got to divide the district into sections for delivery of gasmasks. (*He busies himself at the table with the job.*)

EDGAR
(*ignoring* FEELIM'*s warning*)

Our sun is setting, Drishogue.   What have we young men got to do with the hope and pleasure of a lifetime ?   Where our fathers went, we must go, and whatever sons we may have, will follow us.

DRISHOGUE

Take care, for we may have to wear out ; so be fair to yourself in being fair to Jennie.

EDGAR
(*laughing, with a tinge of bitterness in it*)

How can a man be fair where fair is foul and foul is fair ; when life is a long hover in the fog and the filthy air ? No ; let those who know they die tomorrow be merry today.

[MRS. WATCHIT *comes trotting in carrying a tray on which are a small teapot, covered with a cosy, a cup and saucer, tiny jug of milk, and some sugar in a bowl. She lays it on a table in front of* FEELIM. *She is a woman of fifty, with soft eyes in a lined face ; her hair, almost white, is elaborately permed. She is dressed in bodice and skirt of purple, over which is a small apron trimmed with green. She moves with a slow, stiff trot.*

MRS. WATCHIT
(*beamingly*)
Us knew as you'd like a tot o' tea. 'Usband says as 'ow 'ee thinks as it would buck you up like.

FEELIM
(*with delight*)
Your 'usband's a wise one, me dear lady. Set it down, set it down ; someone must ha' been prayin' for me.

MRS. WATCHIT
(*as she lays it down*)
Shall us pour a cup for 'ee ?

FEELIM
No, no ; not yet. Let it draw an' thicken a little, an' brew. (*He goes on to work, and* MRS. WATCHIT

34

goes out again. With satisfaction — to all in the room) Thoughtful woman, that. Efficient, too. Always doing something, and always doin' it well. (*Musing on the problem*) Division H.I.1, Sub-Division H.I.J.2 ; District O.1.D, Sub-District O.1.D.E ; Section K.L.1, Sub-Section K.L.M.2. Now who th' hell ought to be put there ? I can't see with all these letthers an' integers dazzlin' me.

DRISHOGUE

No, Edgar, though we have more to face than cannon-fire and flak — the frantic wind tearing at our tender house, the hardy, heartless frost flinging his icy coat over us to weigh us down, the lightning's flame stabbing at our entrails, the sea tossing up her highest waves to drench us when we go wounded, limping home ; yet, in spite of all, more than many will never have had their names written down in the little black book ; and, years hence, they will be seen, with shrunken shanks, rheumy eyes, the grey beard and the wasting hair, trying to get their treble voices down to the pitch of youth. (*Speaking a little more slowly*) And even though we should die, then, damn it all, we shall die for a fair cause !

EDGAR
(impatiently)

Oh, all causes are fair to those who believe in them ; I believe in none. I have no cause to die for, such as you love ; no principle ; only an old, doting mother who's jutting close to death her-

35

self : my old and dying mother and myself, but I
cannot die for him.

For England, then.

(*more impatiently*)
Which England ?   There are so many of them :
Conservative England, Liberal England, Labour
England, and your own Communist England —
for which of them shall I go forth to fight, and,
perchance, to die ?

For all of them in the greatness of England's
mighty human soul set forth in what Shakespeare,
Shelley, Keats, and Milton sang ; in the mighty
compass of Darwin's mind, sweeping back to the
beginning and stretching forward to the end ; for
what your Faraday did in taming the lightning to
stream quietly about in the service of man ; and,
if these be indifferent things to you, then fight and
die, if need be, in the halo of healing from the
tiny light carried in the lovely, delicate hands
of Florence Nightingale.   Go forth to fight, perchance to die, for the great human soul of England.
Go forth to fight and to destroy, not the enemies
of this or that belief, but the enemies of mankind.
In this fight, Edgar, righteousness and war have
kissed each other : Christ, Mahomet, Confucius,
and Buddha are one.

EDGAR
(with a sigh)

I daresay you are right. I will, I think, fight
heartily ; but the young love life, and I am young.

DRISHOGUE

And death is but a part of life, my friend. Dying,
we shall not feel lonely, for the great cloud of
witnesses who die will all be young. If death be
the end, then there is nothing ; if it be but a
passage from one place to another, then we shall
mingle with a great, gay crowd !

> [*The dark cloth panel in the wireless cabinet
> suddenly lights up, showing the German
> sign of the swastika in its centre in flaming
> red ; the notes of the first line of " Deutsch-
> land über Alles " are played, and a
> voice, in ordinary confident tones, calls :
> " Germany calling, Germany calling, Ger-
> many calling." Then the swastika dis-
> appears, and the cloth panel of the cabinet
> is dark again.*
>
> *The two young men sit with thoughtful faces,
> their thoughts on themselves ;* FEELIM *sits
> upright, a puzzled, listening look on his
> face. Then he rises, his face a puzzled
> pucker of lines.*

FEELIM

Wha' was that ? (*Without turning — his back is
towards the two young men*) Did yous hear anything ? (*They do not answer.*) Me brain is turning dark an' dazzled with all these problems of

figures, calculations, an' expository confusion of form an' pamphlet. (*He sees the tea.*) Ah! a cup of tea to save a life! It must be well brewed be now. A woman efficient as she is considerate, is Mrs. Watchit. (*He lifts the cosy off, and pours a stream of hot water into the cup, and a look of half-demented disappointment emblazons his face when he realises* MRS. WATCHIT *has forgotten to put in the tea. With an agonised yelp*) Good God! The old fool forgot to put the tea in! Nothing that woman lays a hand on that she doesn't mar. A very pest in the place. She thought of everything but to put in the tea. Escaped her notice. How do they think they're ever goin' to win th' war this way! "*A nice cup o' tea'll tune you up,*" she says; she's tuned me up, right enough, but not with tea. (*He lets an agonised roar out of him.*) Mrs. Watchit! (*He savagely pushes an electric bell near the fireplace. He waits a moment for an answer that doesn't come, then goes over to the doorway, the teapot held out in his hand. Venomously — striding to the doorway*) Gallivantin' afther soldiers, I suppose. They're all at that game. Women of ninety gettin' their hair permed. (*He roars at doorway*) Mrs. Watchit! Mrs. Watchit! (*To the two airmen*) A lovely rest camp this place 'ud make, wouldn't it?

DRISHOGUE
(*annoyed*)

For goodness' sake go down and get the tea, if you want it so bad.

38

FEELIM

(*vehemently*)

I haven't time to stir, man — I've too much to do! (*He gives a long-sustained roar.*) Mrs. Watchit!

[MARK, *the Home Guardsman, in shirt, trousers, and high rubber boots with a pike having a shaft fourteen feet long and a blade two feet long, comes hurrying in, excited and wary.*

MARK

(*excitedly*)

What th' rumble goin' on round here? What's wrong, eh? Quick, show us!

FEELIM

(*as he sees the pike poking about*)

Mind that pike! Mind that pike, there!

MARK

What's amiss? Us heard fierce shoutin' f'rm garden.

FEELIM

(*thrusting teapot towards* MARK)

Nothin's amiss; only bring this back to that woman, Watchit, an' tell her Mr. O'Morrigun would be obliged if she'd thry to make tea in the only way known to mortals. (*As* MARK, *taking hold of teapot, releases hold of pike which crashes over the table*) Mind that pike, I'm tellin' you!

39

MARK

'Tain't no use bringin' teapot down — Mrs. Watchit's gone to market to try ferret out a few eggs.

FEELIM

(*resignedly*)

Then, like a good man, you brew a pot of tea for a man dyin' of drouth.

MARK

That 'tain't no use either. Afore she went, Mrs. Watchit cut off gas from main and put key in pocket to 'usband fuel.

FEELIM

(*madly*)

Oh, is it any wonder revolutions are threatenin' all over the world ! Ah, a wise woman, that Watchit one ! Well, look here, tell Farmer Frome that it'll be hours yet, days, maybe weeks even, before I can give him a hand with the Egg Inspector's report, or the Butter Inspector's report, or the Noxious Weeds Inspector's report, or the Warble Fly Inspector's report.

MARK

(*hesitating*)

Us doesn't like goin' near 'ee. 'Ee's up t' knees in forms, an' is wild-eyed an' roarin'.

FEELIM

Go on — we've all to take risks these days. (*As*

MARK *is going*) Hold on a second ! (*He goes to table, and comes back with a slip of paper in his hand.*) Tell him that a new Ordher, X.123 plus 789, concernin' growers of rhubarb, says, " A grower of rhubarb in relation to, or conception of, the meaning of the order appertaining to the cultivation of live plants or herbs for appropriate culinary purposes, and concerning the growth of the particular herb already specified, or otherwise mentioned, to wit the plant commonly known under the name of rhubarb, is a person set down in the affirmative sense in Form 05321.YX, and includes any person in whom the property in rhubarb is, or has been, invested before its severance thereof from any land in which the said herb, or plant, may be in process of cultivation. For additional information, see Form Y.321, 789.A." Tell that to Farmer Frome from me. It's all about rhubarb.

MARK

Us'll do me best.

> [*He goes out, balancing his pike, and* FEELIM *returns to the table to resume his calculations, carefully replacing, with a sigh, the teapot on the tray.*

DRISHOGUE
(*who for the last few moments has been watching the thoughtful drooping head of* EDGAR)

Come, buddy, come, wake up ! The sheep's in the meadow, the cow's in the corn ! Death never comes so swift as life imagines. And if she comes too swift, why then, The flower that blooms and dies all in a day is fair as one that lingers to decay.

FEELIM
(irritated, and perhaps a little frightened)
Why persevere with this gloomy talk : God's truth, I prefer th' saucy talk of Jennie herself.

DRISHOGUE
However it may be, when we have passed the end, no-one shall know that he is dead ; for still the curlews call, the plovers cry, and linnets sing as sweetly and as loud.

> [*A moment after*, JENNIE *comes tripping in, gay and expectant. She is dressed in her Land Girl walking-out costume — broad-brimmed, brown hat, vivid green jersey, brown breeches, long green-grey stockings, and brown shoes.*

JENNIE
(gaily)
Hello, my merry men all ! (*Coming over to* EDGAR, *and lightly ruffling his hair.*) Come along ; the curfew's tolled the knell of parting day, and Diana's lamp is lit to show a silver path to where we go. (*Seeing how serious they look.*) What th' hell has you all so glum-looking ?

FEELIM
(with dignity)
We were talkin' serious, Jennie.

JENNIE

So am I. What's more serious than the life of this fair world that's in the sidelong glance of a maid at a man ? What were you talkin' about ?

DRISHOGUE

We were talking of death : the fear of it, and how to face it firmly, Jennie.

JENNIE
(*sympathetically — to* EDGAR)

My poor boy ! Were they trying to measure your troubled thoughts with sky-blown rules again ? The best prayers for giving courage and hope are ripe kisses on a young girl's red mouth ! Though life's uncertain, we ought to edge its darkness with a song !

FEELIM

He has a right to be serious when he wants to.

JENNIE

Come on, strong boy. You can be as serious as you like with me. You'll find in me the loaf of bread, the flask of wine, the book of verse, and the maid singing in the wilderness. (*Seizing him by the arm to raise him from his seat*) Up !

EDGAR
(*hesitantly*)

Just a minute, dear ; there's a time for everything.

There's no out-marked hour for love : it is the very breath of time and space.

FEELIM
(*monitorily*)
It's good to think occasionally of God.

JENNIE
(*mockingly*)
Which of them ? There were hundreds. One was in every thunderclap, one flew in every breeze, one lay under every tree ; and now we seek safety in crosses of tin, in a touch of St. Jude's toe, or an eyelash of a St. Camberwell ; forgetting that the stately or nimble song in verse, stone, or picture, and the urge of a young man and woman into each other's arms, are the gay instruments of God's best melodies. (*As* MONICA *enters, dressed for a walk in short skirt, jacket, and blouse, covered by a dark-blue mackintosh*) Ah, dear, we're just in time to deliver our boys from bondage. Get hold of yours, and come along. (*Getting* EDGAR *to his feet, and putting an arm round him*) I'm all cased up in a costume ; but a hand can slip under the jersey, and the girdle's easy undone.

DRISHOGUE
(*slipping an arm round* MONICA *as he goes out with her*)
We'll pull aside shy-buttoned bodice, to glimpse fair perfection beneath.

(*singing saucily*)
She stood where th' primroses blow,
Looking modest an' shy as a daisy ;
Come an' kiss me, sweet maid, said a beau,
Or are you too shy an' too lazy ?

JENNIE
(*as she goes out with* EDGAR)
I can canter like any gee-gee,
Said th' maid to th' man, with a bow, sir ;
An' if you'll be rider to me,
I 'll willingly show you how, now, sir !
[*The couples go out.*
*Outside again can be heard the tramping feet
of the Home Guard drilling ; the non-com.,
or officer in charge, intoning, "* Left. . . .
Left. Into file. . . . Right turn. . . .
Left. . . . Left *"; the distant sound of
the marching feet, distant at first, coming
nearer, till the sound passes by the window,
and moving off, fades away again into the
distance.*

FEELIM
(*clicking his tongue in irritated disdain*)
Dtch dtch ! Boys of the Old Brigade.
[DAME HATHERLEIGH *comes in by the piano on
left. She often has a brisk manner, but
almost always a look of anxiety clouds her
face. She is a woman of forty-five or so,
well figured, though tending, ever so slightly,
towards plumpness. She still holds on to a*

45

good part of an earlier loveliness shown in a heavy mass of brown hair, tinged now with grey specks ; fine, oval face, and eyes, deep, dark, alert, and intelligent, perhaps a little brighter than they should be. She is simply, almost austerely dressed in a tailor-made suit of dark green, relieved by a scarf of deep orange, flecked with crimson round her neck, and a belt of the same colours round her waist.

She is carrying a V-for-Victory sign of white, some two feet in height, which she places upright on the table in its centre. FEELIM *rises, and becomes the obedient and attentive butler at once.*

DAME HATHERLEIGH

Sit down, Feelim ; sit down. You're more important now than I am. (*As she places the V sign on the table*) There's something now to remind all who may be in the room that victory is sure.

FEELIM

It'll be sudden, too, ma'am, never fear.

DAME HATHERLEIGH

I hope so : for my husband's sake and my son's ; for all our sakes. (*With a long and sad sigh.*) It's a bad thing, Feelim, for one's love and hopes to be depending on one child only. (*Her body grows tense, and her face becomes drawn with anxiety and fear, while her eyes stare out in front of her.*)

46

I sometimes dread the things I seem to see and hear, threatening woe to husband and to son. When there is silence in my mind, I see and hear them. (*In a sharper tone*) I see and hear them now : — the cold clang of a horde of tramping jackboots, bound with steel ; the sharp windy scream of a thousand German warplanes, with a pillar of fire moving before them, showing itself in the shape of a whirling swastika ! In the centre of the red fire my son is a perishing white flame ; and the steel-shod jackboots pound down heavy on my husband's body !

[*Before she fancies these things the cloth panel of the wireless cabinet has lit up, showing the bold, brazen sign of the swastika, more clearly than before, and a trumpet sounds confidently, but not loudly, the first line of " Deutschland über Alles ", an aggressive voice proclaims :* " Germany calling, Germany calling, Germany calling ! " *While she speaks, the tramp of many marching feet can be heard, sounding some distance away ; heavier and more rhythmic than the march of the Home Guards, and accompanied with a cold, keen clash, as if every jackboot was shod with steel. The sound does not come near, and fades away when* FEELIM *begins to speak.*

FEELIM
(*encouragingly*)
Both'll be all right, me lady, never fear. It'll all

be over before your son can get his wings.

DAME HATHERLEIGH

He's got them, and so has your Drishogue. I
know, though it isn't official yet : he's got his
wings, but the war isn't over yet.

FEELIM

Both of them'll be all right, ma'am. I know it ;
I feel sure of it.

DAME HATHERLEIGH

It's all in God's hands. All we're sure of is that
England must win : British Israel can never fail.

FEELIM
(*glad to change the subject*)
Never, no ; how could it ?

DAME HATHERLEIGH
(*becoming more eager*)
Isn't it thrilling to feel that we are soul of the soul
of the lost Ten Tribes of Israel, and are being held
firm in the hands of Deity for a special purpose !

FEELIM
(*echoing her elation*)
Thrillin' ? Don't be talkin', me lady !

DAME HATHERLEIGH
(*enthusiastically*)
Heremon's children have a great destiny. (*Suddenly — to* FEELIM) You've heard of Heremon ?

FEELIM

Is it me ? 'Course I have ! Our own ancesthor !

DAME HATHERLEIGH

Yes, our ancestor, the son of a Milesian father
and a Tuatha de Danaan mother, the first of the
line of Zarah, the mother of the line of Dan.

FEELIM
(*echoing*)

Line o' Dan — that's right.

DAME HATHERLEIGH

These are the two tribes who came over with
Simeon of Wales, you know — the ancient Kymri
or Simonii, who were the remnants of the Ten
Tribes, dispersed after the fall of the Assyrian
Empire. (*Ecstatically*) Isn't it wonderful !

FEELIM
(*just as ecstatically*)

There was always somethin' wonderful, somethin'
sthrange, somethin', somethin' thremendous about
th' Irish people !

DAME HATHERLEIGH
(*correcting him*)

British people, Feelim. (*Solemnly and impress-
ively*) We've got to dig, Feelim !

    [MRS. WATCHIT *trots in, looks at them, halts
       a second, and then resumes her trip to the
       table, where she sits down.*

49

FEELIM

(relieved that he knows at last what he is talking about)

You're right there, ma'am. Dig we must while them U-boats are prowlin' about. Dig f'r victory !

DAME HATHERLEIGH

(a little impatiently)

Not that digging ! We must dig for the Ark !

FEELIM

(astounded)

Th' Ark ?

DAME HATHERLEIGH

Oh, Feelim, don't you know that under the Hill of Tara lies the Ark of the Covenant ?

FEELIM

(more astounded than ever)

No !

DAME HATHERLEIGH

Fact. And we must dig it up. The Tara that Heremon gave to his wife as a dowry and burial-place — Teea-Mur — the town of Teea, or Tara as we call it now.

FEELIM

(feelingly)

Home o' th' High Kings ! D'ye know, me lady, I wouldn't be a bit surprised if when you took a top off an Irish mountain, you'd find Noah's Ark restin' in a boggy bed o' moss, with the dove, herself, nestin' near th' tiller !

DAME HATHERLEIGH

We must get the other one first, Feelim. You remember the glorious destiny in store for us, revealed in the Book of Daniel, don't you?

MRS. WATCHIT
(*nodding her head*)

Ay, us knows Daniel.

FEELIM

Daniel? Yes, of course — the fella who fooled about with the lions an' — an' things.

DAME HATHERLEIGH
(*a little impatiently*)

Not the lions, Feelim; the image of brass and gold with the feet of clay that the rock from the mountain cut to pieces in poor Nebuchadnezzar's dream.

FEELIM
(*emphatically*)

Nebuchadnezzar! That's th' fella I've been thryin' to think of — a boyo, if ever there was one.

DAME HATHERLEIGH

It's only when the Stone of Destiny is returned to the Davidic line that Great Britain and America will become one happy and united family, having one baptism, and holding one faith. Mind you, it's no myth, Feelim.

51

MRS. WATCHIT
(*nodding head*)

No, no myth ; all on us knows Nebuchadnezzar.

FEELIM

Myth is it ? I'd like to meet th' one would say it was ! Didn't I see it all with me own eyes, an' I in the Royal Irish Academy one day, written down in th' Tawny Deeds of th' Triads of Tirawly, set down in the sixth century before Anno Domini. It's only too thrue. Th' only throuble is, me lady, in this unbelievin' age, you'll get few to stand for Nebuchadnezzar's Dream, or th' image, or th' Ten Thribes, or even th' noble lady, Teeaa, who gave her name to Tara.

DAME HATHERLEIGH

You're forgetting the Ark of the Covenant, Feelim : confront them with that, and they'd be speechless.

FEELIM
(*earnestly*)

You're right, they would — speechless, be God, they'd be, sure enough !

DAME HATHERLEIGH
(*with ecstatic fanaticism*)

The moment the war ends, we'll set about it ; dig briskly, but ever reverently. You know Tara, Feelim ?

FEELIM
(*as enthusiastically*)

Every green sod of it, me lady !

52

Well, when you've time, sketch out a detailed plan
of the hill, so that we may know where it is best to
excavate first — when you've time. And now to
war work — I to the Red Cross Committee, and,
after that, the provision of billets for the aerodrome workers ; and you ?

FEELIM

(*indicating* MRS. WATCHIT)

We're just about to measure our light an' fuel
expenditure so's to keep future records.

DAME HATHERLEIGH

Patriotic work, my dears. (*She bends to whisper*)
When Mr. Edgar returns, say I want to see him.
Goodbye for the present.

    [*She goes out.* FEELIM *rises, goes over, opens
        the door for her, and bows as gracefully as
        any eighteenth-century courtier.*

FEELIM

(*as soon as the door is shut — raising his eyes
to the ceiling*)

Didja hear that rigmarole ! Dig out Tara, she
says, to find th' Ark of the Covenant. Think of
your sthrong connection, says she, with the lost
Ten Thribes. Abraham, Isaac, an' Jacob, I know,
were three of them, but th' names of th' others
has escaped me memory.

MRS. WATCHIT

Us'll ask 'usband — 'ee's sure t'know.

53

Ah, for God's sake, let th' mania stay with one, and don't spread it on to others! Is it outa me mind she thinks I am, or what? What d'ye take me for, woman, says I? Won't we be tired enough when we're done diggin' for victory, without breakin' our backs diggin' up Tara's Hill? Wouldn't I look a nice gazebo shovin' th' Ark of th' Covenant through the streets of Dublin or of Cork? I can hear th' people laughin' from here! If I was caught diggin' there, they'd ask, What are you diggin' for, Feelim? Th' Ark of the Covenant, I'd say, what else? Th' what? he'd say; an', when I woke, yours truly would find himself in a padded cell.

MRS. WATCHIT

Dame Hatherleigh's a good woman, an' kind, all upset by Mr. Edgar lowerin' himself goin' with that Jennie Frome; an' her poor mind whirlin' by actin' secretary to seven committees.

FEELIM
(savagely)

You keep your mind from whirlin' when you're makin' tea; an' when you make it, make it with tea, and don't thry to make it with a miracle!

MRS. WATCHIT
(realising)

Us knew us had forgotten something! Us'll run down an' slip on kettle for another, while you

lay out plans. Lady was 'ere again, lookin' for
Drishogue.

> [*She whips up tray of things, and runs out.
> Clearing his throat with some short coughs,
> a lot of hems and haws,* FEELIM *clears a
> space on the table, and arranges on it a
> thick exercise-book, a sheaf of writing
> paper, a bunch of pencils, and a pen and ink.
> He sits down, and begins to pore over the
> dial plans of the gas and electric meters.*
> MRS. WATCHIT *returns, trotting over to his
> side, and bending down to see what* FEELIM
> *has arranged. They straighten their backs,
> and carefully put on their spectacles, with
> some more short coughs and hems and haws.*

FEELIM
(*confidently*)

Now, we're all set, an' do thry to keep your mind
from whirlin'. Now here's th' plan of the electric
dial. Yes ; yes. Now, there's three dials, no,
four ; no, five dials altogether.

MRS. WATCHIT

Us thought us counted six.

FEELIM

One's a test dial, an' no concern of ours. One ten
thousand, one thousand, one hundred, one ten,
and one one — five altogether. See ?

MRS. WATCHIT

See what ?

55

I mean, understand ?

But unnerstand what ?

(*sharply*)
Five dials, ma'am, showin' th' amounts of electricity we're consumin'.

I says t' my 'usband, us says to 'ee, I says five dials I says — fancy !

Let's get to the units — tens o' thousands, thousands, hundreds, an' ones. Now let's see what it says, keeping th' units in our heads.

'Usband says to me, five dials 'ee says ; an' another red one, says us to 'ee ; fancy, now, says 'ee, why, 'ee says, suppose they does it to puzzle folks.

Wait a minute. What we have to do is to subtract th' amount of currency shown today——

Add it, isn't it ? 'Usband says t' us amount used since before we see'd last figure, 'ee says, must be

added t' quantity, 'ee says, consumed, previous t'
calculation made at first.

FEELIM
(*beginning to be annoyed — imitating her*)
Listen, ma'am — 'ee says 'ere— (*he taps the plan
sharply with a finger*)—'ee says, " Read your
meter ; take down th' total on the dials," 'ee says.
          [MARK *peeps into the room from the doorway.*

MARK
Any chance of spot of tea for us an' mates ?

FEELIM
(*annoyed — gesturing for him to go away*)
We're busy, now, we're busy !

MRS. WATCHIT
(*waving him away*)
Checkin' our 'lectricity ; mustn't think of tea
now.   Us's on war work.

MARK
(*coming over to the table on tiptoe, and cautiously
          bending over to watch the work*)
Them dials is enough to fair dazzle a man proper.

MRS. WATCHIT
(*nodding her head in assent*)
Dials work contrary, too — a hand goin' left, a
hand goin' right, an' t' other movin' left.

What's Government athinkin' of ?   Drill, I says,
yes, night an' day, manœuvrin', trench diggin',
an' camoflage crawlin', all fair an' square, I says,
is what us wants, to be ready to stick parachute
Jerries droppin' about, I says, outa clouds, afore
he lands, with day's work an' snatch o' sleep,
enough t' go round clock, without shovin' of
things forward us doesn't know how t' do.

FEELIM
(*indignantly*)

Who says he doesn't know how ?   Jot down
figures the dials show, and a computation between
the figures, here and there, and you get your
answer ; but what can a man do with a thunder
of talk in his ear ?

MICHAEL
(*popping his head in by the doorway*)

Any chance o' thet spot o' tea, Mark ?

FEELIM
(*clicking his tongue in annoyance*)

Dtch dtch !

MRS. WATCHIT
(*waving him away*)

We're too busy now.   Us's on war work !

MARK
(*warningly — to* MICHAEL)

Hshush !   Us's questionin' th' dials.

[MICHAEL *tiptoes over to the table to join the
group bending over the plans. He is short,
stout, bull-necked ; and he gasps a little
after every sentence.*

MRS. WATCHIT

Us's all tryin' t' help, no more. 'Usband says only
way t' live, 'elp one another, 'ee says, spite of dis-
comforts, denials, an' suchlike hazards, till day
breaks an' shadows flee away.

MICHAEL

All sound, Christian doctrine, sensible, too, us'll
all agree.

FEELIM
(*with icy anger*)

We're not concerned now with sound Christian
doctrine, good people, but with secular instruments ticking out problems it takes concentration
to solve.

MARK

Best way conserve fuel, I says, is keep aturnin'
down gas-tap, don't light fires, keep poker locked
up, mark time with hot water, riddle-me-ree
th' ashes, an' don't light no light that 'tisn't
necessary.

FEELIM
(*mockingly*)

And never get outa bed ! What we've got to do is
to find the kilowatt-hours an' th' job's done.

MICHAEL

Aay, find 'em, but that's hard as what they calls asplittin' of that there addem.

MRS. WATCHIT

(*nodding her head in profound assent*)

'Tis that; though it's all a knack, asplittin' of the addem, or ferretin' out them vitamins, 'usband said tonight, a week ago, comin' from Three Pigeons — once get th' knack, 'ee says, an' everythin's no more'n openin' door an' shuttin' she behind you.

FEELIM

(*emphatically*)

Keep silent, th' lot of you, or go away, till I set me mind on these figures.

[*A jet of dirty steam streams suddenly in through the doorway.*

MARK AND MICHAEL

(*together — alarmed*)

Th' house afire, or somethin'!

MRS. WATCHIT

(*aghast — springing to her feet,*

The kettle for th' tea! God! Us forgot th' 'lectric kettle on stove!

[*She trots madly out, followed by* MARK *and* MICHAEL.

FEELIM

(*in agony*)

Th' current, the current! Waste, waste! A year

won't save what we've lost today in half an hour !
(*The big door flies open, and* MONICA, *pursued by*
DRISHOGUE, *runs in. He catches her half-way
across the room, presses her in his arms, and kisses
her hotly several times. Leaning back in his chair,
exhausted*) I dunno, I dunno ; instead of gettin'
them down, th' war seems to be gettin' them all
hit up !

MONICA
(*breathless — striving to free herself*)
Please, Drishogue, I must take the class ; they're
waiting. It is very important ; it may separate
life from death at grips in some wounded body to
meet one quick to fix a pad, a bandage, or a
tourniquet — let me go !

DRISHOGUE
(*releasing her*)
Tonight, then, for it's a dark joy to have to leave
you now.

MONICA
Yes ; tonight !
[*She runs out, and* DRISHOGUE *flings himself
into chair*, FEELIM *watching him reprovingly.*

FEELIM
For goodness' sake go a little more orderly —
we're not in Russia now.

DRISHOGUE
Wish to God we were.

61

FEELIM
(*sarcastically*)
Perfection there, eh ?

DRISHOGUE
Far from it ; only a hard, bitter, glorious struggle
towards it.

> [MRS. WATCHIT *comes in by the big door ; she
> is wearing an air of importance, and she
> is followed by* JOY *and another Land Girl,
> both of whom are in walking-out uniform; a
> member of the A.T.S., one of the W.A.A.F.,
> a Girl Warden, and* MARK.

MRS. WATCHIT
(*to* FEELIM — *beamingly*)
Us was just in time to save house fr'm fire ! (*To*
DRISHOGUE) A very talented young lady, an Em
Ah an' all . . . wants t' have a word with 'ee.

FEELIM
(*sitting straight in his chair — to* DRISHOGUE)
An Em Ah an' all.   Came several times. (*To*
DEEDA) Here he is, ma'am.

> [MRS. DEEDA TUTTING *comes strutting towards*
> DRISHOGUE *through the lane formed by the
> others.   She is a tall, gaunt, plain-faced
> woman of forty or so.   Her hair, turning
> grey slowly, is rather untidy, with wisps
> hanging down her neck and over her ears.
> Deep clefts connect a very querulous mouth*

with the butt of a thick and aggressive nose.
Her forehead stretches too far back, giving
her face a longer look than it really has.
She is wearing big, round, horn-rimmed
glasses, and carries a big, loose-bodied,
black handbag, bulging with papers. She
is dressed in a vivid green skirt, blue blouse,
and thick-soled brogues. A black kerchief,
striped with white, encircles her neck.
Her voice is loud, rather shrill, and her
manner positive and dogmatic.

MRS. WATCHIT
(*with all possible refinement — introducing her*)
Us has great pleasure in introducin' Mrs. Deeda
Tutting.

DEEDA
(*thrusting out a big hand which* DRISHOGUE
shakes gloomily and warily — with dogmatic
familiarity)
Hello there ! So you're the young man who
adores the Soviet Union ? I don't blame you :
Lenin began well, and we all had hopes for
Russia's future ; but that's a lost dream now !

FEELIM
Hear that, now, Drishogue ?

MRS. WATCHIT
Us always had suspicions.

63

I and my husband worked there on Committees, Comintern and Light Industries, so I know. If you were there, you'd see a look of fear in every sunken eye, misery chiselled on every pallid face, rags trying to cling to every shrunken body, and all steeped in the drab life they have to live.

DRISHOGUE

Others with eyes as clear as yours, lady, have seen brighter and manlier things there. The fear you say you saw may have been the deep, dark fire of courage ; the chiselled lines in pallid faces, the insignia of resolution ; the ragged garments, the hurried shelter worn by sturdy hope striding down the street. If you want, woman, to see fear in th' eye, the pinched and pallid face, the shrunken figure, the tattered garment, ribbed to welcome every gusty wintry wind, look here at home — you'll find them plentiful in every town and city !

DEEDA

(*more shrill and positive*)

Can't you listen ? I know !

FEELIM

Listen to the lady, son, who has had experience. Things happen when th' world turns from God.

DEEDA

My husband worked beside me. He, too, found his dream was false. (*With a shrill and positive*

whine.)   He suddenly disappeared like thousands
of others — perhaps millions — into a concentration camp.   (*In a modified scream*.)   If it
weren't for you and other Liberals here, Stalin
daren't have done it !

DRISHOGUE
(*mockingly*)
You'll be telling me in a minute that Stalin himself is the one man left outside a concentration
camp !

FEELIM
Odd things happen, Drishogue, when th' people
turn from God.
[MICHAEL *rushes in, excited and angry, and
pushes his way to* FEELIM, *waving a big
official form in his hand*.

MICHAEL
Ere, looka, read this one !

MRS. WATCHIT
(*warningly*)
Shush, man, we're talkin' serious.

MICHAEL
(*ignoring her — loudly*)
Government, she says, will acquire total egg
output of keepers of thirteen hens or more, at
thruppence an egg, 'n us's spent a tenner or more
on hencoop an' fowl-run !

65

JOY
(*angrily — to* MICHAEL)

Can't you see us's in middle of important discussion ?

MICHAEL
(*persistent*)

An' th' balance of meal allowed for fowl is same f'r twelve as f'r twenty, so's plain owner of twenty uses no more'n 'im of twelve, so's owner of twenty is consumin' no more'n owner of twelve's, so's his balance o' meal's no more'n owner of twelve's, so why penalise one more'n other by she makin' compulsory purchase of egg output ? (*Indignantly*) Us'll not stick it !

FEELIM
(*to* DEEDA)

Go on, lady ; never mind him.

DEEDA
(*tearfully continuing her story*)

Arrested without a word, without a sign, my poor husband's dead by now for certain. Listen : (*She bangs the table with her fist.*) They lay hands on whom they like to send them to forced labour. What can your subtle Irish mind say to that, eh ?

DRISHOGUE
(*calmly*)

Well, if the behaviour you're showing now is usual with you, I don't wonder your husband disappeared — it was the wisest thing he could do.

FEELIM

(*reproachfully while* DEEDA *stands silent,*
viciously looking at DRISHOGUE)

Aw now, Drishogue, aw now ! Th' Gestapo took him, Drishogue ; th' Gestapo took him.

JOY

Who else, I ask ?

DEEDA

(*to* FEELIM)

The Ogpu, sir, not the Gestapo. (*To* DRISHOGUE — *violently*) I tell you, young man, the National Socialism of Germany, in many respects, is far superior to Soviet Rule ; and if it only gives up its racial animosity, and its spirit of conquest, it's Germany will become more cultured than even Britain's or France's pompous and hypocritical imperialism !

DRISHOGUE

You're asking a lot of Fascism, lady — you're asking it to cease to be itself.

DEEDA

(*furiously*)

Germany has as much right to *Lebensraum* as we have, and peace with her is the one chance of saving ourselves ; for if America and England war with Germany, it may well bring about a fusion of Hitlerism and Stalinism into one mighty movement of destruction !

MICHAEL

(*violently breaking out again*)

What about a little *Lebensraum* for decent people's hens ! What's use of blamin' governments away off when our own at home's worse ?

FEELIM

(*angrily*)

You don't know what you're sayin', man !

MICHAEL

Well, us knows what us's sayin', but no one wants t' listen t' uns. Us'll soon 'ave Inspectors be'ind every bush watchin' hens layin'. What's become of that 'ere Magna Charta, us asks ?

FEELIM

(*indignantly*)

Good God, man, can't you realise there's a lady speakin' ? Can't you realise that your hens and everyone's hens an' cocks are insignificant things compared with the tremendous thruths this lady is enunciatin' ?

JOY

(*solemnly*)

Nothin' can prevail against truth.

DRISHOGUE

(*to* DEEDA)

There must be something great in what the rank and gaudy privilege of the world's power, secular and clerical, is afraid of : but this great people know only a rational fear, for at the top of their resolution is the spearhead of their Red Army.

DEEDA

(*wheeling round to face the crowd*)

Are you listening to this miserable, besotted, and belated nonsense ! (*She wheels round to face* DRISHOGUE *again.*) Don't be a fool, man ! I've seen them, and I know — a deformed, ill-nourished, tatter-clad crowd ! Their rifles are soft-tube toys ; the wings of their warplanes fall off in a sturdy wind ; their big guns melt away after a few shots ; and their tanks crumple into scrap when they strike a stone in the roadway !

DRISHOGUE

(*sarcastically*)

They do, do they ? What a pity !

MRS. WATCHIT

(*nodding her head in assent*)

Us guessed it all along.

DEEDA

(*carried away — almost screaming*)

Behind your boasting façade of Soviet achievement lies a chaos of incompetence, a mass of sullen terror, a swamp of ignorance ; at war, your Red Army will be so stupidly led and so wretchedly supplied that it will scatter from the field in utter rout before a month of war has passed. (*She bends down till her face is close to that of* DRISHOGUE.)   And I will be glad, delighted, overjoyed at its overthrow !   If there is any honesty or truth left in us, we'll be at war with them soon to sweep away the horrid falsity of them and their master !

DRISHOGUE
(*springing to his feet — fiercely and loudly*)
Woe unto any nation making war on the Soviet Union !   She will slash open the snout, and tear out the guts of any power crossing her borders !

DEEDA
(*coldly*)
Nice language, I must say !

3RD HOME GUARD
(*shouting in from doorway*)
Sarge, Captin's callin' for 'ee all over place !

MICHAEL
(*answering back as loudly*)
Let 'im — us 'as to see 'bout 'ens !

DRISHOGUE
(*fiercely still*)
The people cannot stop for you to catch them up ; if you can't go fast enough to keep in step, then pray for death, for you've lost a use for life !

FEELIM
(*as fiercely as* DRISHOGUE)
Remember the lady's a lady, man, an' an Em Ah,

too ! It's that Red Dean an' his book that has turned your mind asthray. He didn't tell you that four-sixths of his sixth of a Socialist world was naught but snow an' ice an' frozen soil, where no animal plays, no bird flies, no creatures crawl, no man can live ; naught but stunted birch, a biting, bitter wind, an' endless night where shivering Death himself stands idle and alone !

DRISHOGUE

(*to* DEEDA — *fiercely*)

You waste God's time and mine, woman. Over in the east, the people took their first fine step forward, and they look over the rim of the world now. Many can see them clearly, and many more can hear them cheering. We know full well the hardships all before us. Our spring will still have many a frosty morning and a frosty night ; our summers hot hold many a burden for us ; our autumn glory will still be tinged with many a starless night, the sound of sorrow loud beneath their shrouded silence ; but winter's night of hopeless woe is gone forever, and the people's energetic joy shall sound like well-cast bells through every passing season !

DEEDA

(*furiously*)

You seem to be unspeakably intolerant ! I must say I cannot understand the mystery of the Irish mind.

71

DRISHOGUE

There you show your weakness. (*Pointing to* FEELIM) His mind's as Irish as mine, yet you understand it well.

DEEDA
(*beyond herself*)

I tell you the workers in the Soviet Union are worse than ever they were ; and you must be a starry-eyed sucker not to see it !

FEELIM
(*angrily*)

An' add to that her poor husband bein' whipped away to a lingerin' death be th' Gestapo !

DEEDA
(*to* FEELIM — *angrily*)

How often have I to tell you ? Not the Gestapo, you old fool — the Ogpu !

> [DEEDA's *venomous remark half stuns* FEELIM, *and while he is staring at her, the globe over the clock shines into a vivid purple light.*
>
> DAME HATHERLEIGH *enters briskly, but stops, and stands still to watch, and listen to, the disputants, a look of indignation on her face. She is in fire-fighting dress. The cloth panel of the · wireless cabinet is illumined with the swastika, the trumpets play " Deutschland über Alles " ; but the animated crowd take notice of nothing but themselves.*

FEELIM

*(recovering from the shock — while the
trumpets are sounding)*

I think you're after makin' a mistake, madam ;
while you may be no lady, I'm no fool !

DEEDA
(with irritation)

Oh ! be silent, please ! I'm not concerned with
you — (*pointing to* DRISHOGUE) I'm addressing
this young man here.

FEELIM
(angrily)

Well, I'm addressing you ! You're no messenger
from Mars in th' guise of a lady born an' bred,
causin' commotion with tawdry stories of starvin'
shadows slinkin' through crooked streets, dis-
appearin' husbands, armies formed o' scarecrows,
till our brains are dizzy — well, here's one,
anyway, who doesn't believe you ever seen a
sthreak o' sunlight shinin', or a snowflake fall, on
Soviet soil !

DAME HATHERLEIGH
(with quiet indignation)

Oh, you pack of glittering daws ! There you
crowd bickering while death, in a moment, is
certain for some, grievous injury for many, and
terror for us all ! Look at the purple light !
Set out the splints, bandages, and pads ; see to
the incendiary fire tools ; and man the stirrup-
pumps.

FEELIM
(*alert in an instant — putting on equipment*)
To our posts — all of us !
[*All but the* DAME, DRISHOGUE, *and* FEELIM *go
out in different ways.*

DRISHOGUE
Where can I go, Dad ?   What can I do ?

DAME HATHERLEIGH
(*putting a hand on his shoulder*)
Find the safest shelter you can — we shall need
you for finer and more terrible work before long.

DRISHOGUE
Where's Monica ?

DAME HATHERLEIGH
At her post.
[FEELIM, *having put on his steel hat and other
equipment, goes out with* DAME HATHER-
LEIGH *as the warning siren is wailing,
while* DRISHOGUE *stares out of the window.*

END OF ACT I

ACT II

[*The* SCENE *is the same as before, but it is early morning with a nip of frost in the air; the birds are beginning their preliminary chittering and the crows their cawing, before the day's work, and a cock crows afar off. The lights are on for the black-out has to remain up for some time yet.* JOY, *in full working dress of the Land Girl, is waiting by the door for* JENNIE *who is coquettishly arranging her bright-coloured kerchief around her handsome head.*

JENNIE
(*shivering a little*)

God, it's cold! You'd never think so many birds would be so near a town.

JOY

Six hours alert lasted. Thank goodness none came near'n five miles away. Duxton got it hot. Was you nervous?

JENNIE

Hardly, dear. It was a godsend to me. With all out on duty, and too tired to move when they came back, it meant a glorious night of fulfilling a feminine duty with Edgar.

JOY
(*giggling*)

Same 'ere with Sergeant Mark.

75

JENNIE

That's the fitter on the aerodrome works ? Clever
fellow, me lass ; keep tight hold on 'im.

JOY
(*giggling, but trying to be solemn*)

Us 'as more'n us can do t' keep 'im fr'm keepin'
tight 'old of me ! Us never knew till las' night
how unruly 'ee could be.

JENNIE

Nice, but naughty. Ruffled you a lot, eh ?

JOY

God forgive uns all ! (*With prim piety*) 'Taint
right, somehow. What if us caused a curse on all
us's doin' ? Fine thing if harvest failed, an' all
them U-boats sinkin' ships on sea !

JENNIE
(*impatiently*)

Oh, come off it, Joy ! Don't be trying to afflict
us with the old wife's tale of the knife, the victim
tied to an altar, waiting for fire from heaven to
set alight the logs below it. The stormy night of
your harum-scarum god is over. Don't be afraid
when your hair gets tangled in the stem and leaf
of the myrtle.

JOY

Hurry up, dear ; I can hear th' other girls waitin'
below for us.

JENNIE

(*opening bureau, and rummaging about in it*)

Christ ! if anyone told me a year ago I'd be up
at dawn to plant, to mow, to reap, and to sow, and
to be a farmer's boy, I'd have brained him with
his lady's fan ! Ah ! here it is — behind the
bible. (*She takes out a bottle of gin and two
glasses, pouring some gin into each.*) Now the
dawn won't appear so dangerous. (*She hands a
glass to the giggling* JOY.) To the old Dame and
all her Ten Tribes !

[*She and* JOY *drink the gin.*

JOY

All th' same us is anxious. D'ye think th'
Jerries'll invade 'ere ? We're not far f'm th'
coast.

JENNIE
(*carelessly*)

We'll stick it if they do.

JOY

What would you do if they come ?

JENNIE

Live on if I can ; die in my lover's arms, or die
fighting them, if I can't.

GIRLS' VOICES
(*outside*)

Eh, you two — hurry up !

77

JENNIE
(*shouting back*)

Eager for work, what ! (*To* JOY) Another before
we entice ourselves out into the cold. (*She fills
glasses again, giving one to* JOY, *and holding on to
the second herself. She raises the glass on high,
and sings ; drinking the gin when she finishes the
verse :*)

Oh, here's to the trousers and green jersey, too,
That are out in the sun, the rain, and the dew.
Under the sky when it's black or it's blue,
Digging hard, digging deep, in the morning !

(*Girls, chorusing outside, while* JENNIE *shoves back
bottle and glasses into the bureau :*)

GIRLS

Maiden that's bashful, and maiden who's bold,
Forget all th' tales about love ever told ;
And think of your toiling on farm and in wold,
Digging hard, digging deep, in the morning !

JENNIE
(*singing*)

Make way for the Land Girls true, and as
    brave
As soldier in battle, or seaman on wave ;
Giving back in her work some of what Eng-
    land gave,
Digging deep, digging hard, in the morning !

> [JENNIE *and* JOY, *having switched off the light,
> go out, and, with the other girls, can be
> heard singing the chorus of the song, till it
> dies away in the distance.*

*After a few moments, a beam of light comes in
from the doorway, followed by* MONICA *who
is holding a torch in her hand. She is
dressed in a white nightgown, slashed with
blue on the shoulders, a black dressing-
gown, with blue trimmings almost covering
it. Dark-blue slippers cover her bare feet.*

MONICA
*(turning towards the doorway, after switching
on a light)*

There they go, singing to their work. After last
night's worry, the rest won't rise for a little longer.
[DRISHOGUE *comes in now, dressed in his Air
Force uniform, the new white wings sparkling on his breast. He is buttoning his coat,
and his shoes remain unlaced. He is a
little shy and awkward-looking.*

MONICA
(rallying him)

Don't look so glum, dear. We haven't done anything so terrible as you may do before long : isn't
it nobler to bring one life into the world than to
hunt a hundred out of it ?

DRISHOGUE

Depends on the kind you kill. Besides, I don't
want a scene — your father going for you because
you're gone on me, and mine for me because I'm
gone on you.

MONICA

What they say or do down in a hollow matters little to what we say or do up on a hill. Oh, Drishogue, darling, I am very anxious! I'm always thinking of you passing in your plane, the countless flaming fingers of death clutching at you, as you fly by, to pull you down! Don't you fear it, too?

DRISHOGUE
(*thoughtfully*)

No, not fear; a little nervous at the forging of a will into a new adventure.

MONICA
(*shuddering*)

I wish I could keep away from the thoughts of death: were you to go, I should be a desolate little ship lost on a lonely sea.

DRISHOGUE

It is inevitable we should think of what is everywhere around us.

MONICA
(*clinging to him*)

Oh, Drishogue, surely death cannot mean the loss of life!

DRISHOGUE

Perhaps not; I only know it means the loss of many lovely things: the moving patterns of flying birds; the stroll through crowded streets, crudely strewn about, that the moon regenerates

into silvered haunts of meditative men ; the
musical wile of waves racing towards us, or slowly
bidding us farewell ; the wild flowers tossing
themselves on to the field and into the hedgerow ;
the sober ecstasy, or jewelled laugh, of children
playing ; the river's rowdy rush or graceful
gliding into sea or lake ; the sun asthride the hills,
or rainfall teeming down aslant behind them ;
a charming girl, shy, but ready with her finest
favours — oh, these are dear and lovely things
to lose !

MONICA

They may be shadows of finer things to come.

DRISHOGUE

Give me but these, and God can keep whatever
is behind them. But let us get away before the
others come. We ought to go before the house
awakens.

MONICA

(*a little impatiently*)

Oh, let them come ! To be afraid of what we've
done is to be like a young oak shivering in a
summer breeze. Sometimes a quiet life becomes
too precious to us all. Why should you fear the
taunt in the rosy hours spent with the girl you
like ?

DRISHOGUE

And love, too, darling.

MONICA

For the time being, anyway.

81

Till time has grown so old that things remembered
lose their colour, and are growing grey.

MONICA

Dark woe to think how things have changed so
sudden ! (*In the distance, they hear faintly the
drilling of the Home Guard in the rhythmic
murmur of* " Left right, left right, left right.")
Drill on, drill on, Home Guard, first thing at
morning, last thing at night, for England sorely
needs you now ; for France is gone, and England's good right arm hangs helpless by her side !

DRISHOGUE

And you must be as the Irish lass of twice a
hundred years ago, who sold her rock and sold
her reel and sold her only spinning-wheel, to buy
her love a sword of steel to fix him fitly in the
fight for the rights of man.

MONICA

I'll have to do it soon enough ; but first come,
love, to my room again, to dream away from us a
moment more of restless turnings to the sound of
war ; and give darkness another chance to hush
a lover and his lass into the sweet secrecy of
themselves.

[*He goes to the window, pulls down a blackout, and looks out.*

DRISHOGUE

I ought to go before the house awakens. Look !

the moon is pale and worn after dancing through the sky as the beauty of the night, and is bidding goodbye at the door of dawn.

MONICA

False dawn, with hate in all it's lovely face! (*Suddenly the window is shaken, and the house trembles.*) God, what's that!

DRISHOGUE

Blast, I suppose, from a distant bomb exploding.

MONICA
(*shivering*)
They sometimes say that this old house is haunted.

DRISHOGUE
(*merrily*)
You're as superstitious as my father, who, if he had his way, would have my neck ajingle with his holy medals. (*He opens the window.*) That was no ghostly tremor. Let the light o' day come in to banish the shadows of the mind's imagining. There now's the enlivening air of the morning, bringing with it, too, the innocent, elegant scent of lavender.

MONICA
(*a little hysterical*)
Not lavender!   Anything but lavender!

DRISHOGUE
(*dreamily*)
It is mixed with the air stealing in through the

window from the mauvy blossoms of the plant outside.

MONICA

There's none outside ; none, I tell you ! It's your imagination. It's musk, or myrtle, or mignonette that scents the air to touch our senses with a silent sadness.

DRISHOGUE
(*quietly insistent*)

It's lavender, When we sheltered in your room, it was there ; and it has followed us here.

MONICA
(*clinging to him*)

Drishogue, my love, do not seek the centre of danger, but keep warily to the fringe of fighting ! Though I should never have seen you, had you not come to us, I sometimes wish you hadn't ventured into danger for the love of England !

DRISHOGUE
(*starting away from her — with startled indignation*)

Love of England ! Good God, woman, I have no love for England !

MONICA
(*startled too*)

But aren't you fighting for her ?

DRISHOGUE
(*passionately*)

No, I'm not ! I'm fighting for the people. I'm

84

fighting against the stormy pillagers who blackened the time-old walls of Guernica, and tore them down ; who loaded their cannon in th' name of Christ to kill the best men Spain could boast of ; who stripped the olive groves and tore up orange trees to make deep graves for men, heaping the women on the men, and the children on the women. I was too young then to go out armed for battle, but time has lengthened an arm long enough to pull the Heinkels and the Dorniers out of the sky, and send them tumbling down to hell !

MONICA
(*soothingly*)

There, there ! I meant no harm, and, anyway, I'm not an English girl, but a thoroughbred Cornish lass.

DRISHOGUE
(*delightedly*)

A Kelt ! How well I knew some jewel of nature hid in how you looked and what you did and all you said ! A Keltic kiss for my Cornish girl. (*He kisses her.*)

MONICA

But Jennie Frome's English, Drishogue, and you like her well.

DRISHOGUE

I like her well, but are you sure she's English ?

MONICA

She's English right enough.

DRISHOGUE
(*doubtfully*)

I don't know. You search back far enough, and
you'll find some Kymric, Scottish, or Irish
ancestor who has saved her soul alive. (*Whip-
ping her up in his arms with a wild movement*)
Now for another wild welcome to my own dear
Cornish lass ! (*As he bears her out, the house
shivers again, and the windows shake. He stops,
and lets her slide from his arms. Awed.*) There it
is again — the house is quivering over us ! And
there goes the scent of lavender again — no
longer coy — but the scent of lavender a long
time dead !

MONICA
(*frightened*)

Oh, come away, for God's sake !

[ABRAHAM   PENRHYN — MONICA'S   *father —
        appears at the window. He is a moist-eyed,
        high-foreheaded man of fifty or more. His
        bushy grizzled hair, longer at the back than
        it ought to be for a farmer, is strictly
        brushed back from his forehead. A long,
        grizzled beard flows from his chin down
        over his breast ; he would look venerable
        but for the thin-lipped mouth, and the
        stern and unhappy wrinkled lines at each
        corner of it. When he climbs into the room,
        he is seen to be dressed in brown corduroy
        trousers, tight brown leggings, heavy black
        boots, thick brown tweed coat, with a cap of
        same colour and material on his grizzled*

head. For a moment or two he stares at the couple, and a look of silent and bitter anger spreads over his face.

ABRAHAM

You be there, ah, yes ; the two of ye ; full o' th' malice of sin ; thought, word, an' deed conspirin' to flare out in opposition t' God's commandments ! Worse 'n all, too, encompassed by th' arms of a man o' war. Things is bad f'r a once innocent girl sunk down on th' breast of a man o' blood. All th' wonders o' creation, all mercies o' grace, all glory of un eternal future set as naught against a dream of lasciviousness. Is it a wonder house trembles ? No more be a flood of water, God's promise holds ; but a flood o' flame may burn th' world, for the evil's great, un th' time favourable. (*He climbs over sill, and comes into the room.*) Are ye daughter o' mine, or be ye some shamed shadow, stuffed wi' venom against th' good ye cannot own yourself ?

MONICA
(storming into dialect)

Shamed body I am to have to call such a shape as you a feyther !

ABRAHAM

What of your mother in her grave ? (*Almost screaming.*) What of your dear mother, I says ! Wrigglin' in agony in her abode of bliss she are to see you slinkin' off an' slidin' down away off afar from she un' God t' where th' means of sin float thick as semmer swerms of gayly-banded bees, their colours hidin' stings !

MONICA
(*fiercely*)

Don't 'ee jerk name o' mother from th' very rest that cries shame at 'ee, f'r 'ee never raised she higher 'n her knees ! She hurried there t' hide fr'm 'ee. A coloured kerchief on head, a wee brooch on breast to 'ee were signs fr'm Satan aseekin' out her soul !

ABRAHAM
(*vehemently*)

So they was, an' so they does remain ! But f'r us'n timely warnin's, she'd ha' been as you is now. Be ye me daughter, or be ye not, 'tisn't f'r us t' say, for ye have no look about ye of a decent bringin'-up !

DRISHOGUE
(*catching* MONICA's *arm*)

Monica, come away, come away !

MONICA
(*fiercely — shaking his hand away*)

Not since mother left 'ee for ever, when I was ten, ha' I been near you as daughter or friend, and am no more ; no, never. Dame Hatherleigh has had to do me f'r mother an' f'r feyther since. (*More fiercely*) Get away from me ; get far away from me lover 'n me !

ABRAHAM

(with bitter reproach)

Us fattened bullocks for she an' 'ee, didn' I ?
An' reared sheep, an' ploughed land, an' sowed
corn, an' watched sun, rain, an' worked, waitin',
watchin' crops agrowin' f'r 'ee an' she ; t' furnish
roof over heads, meat f'r table, an' clothes f'r
backs, didn' I ? An' now to know taste of what
'ee do an' what 'ee thinks, us 'as to steal along at
nights, un' in the dawn ; steal an' creep afther 'ee
t' end up in seein' of 'ee near t' nakedness in arms
of man of war ! *(Violently)* No daughter of
mine ; no, never, even f'r 'ee to go on bended
knee, un' ask forgiveness !

MONICA

(violently)

Get away fr'm me ; away, far away fr'm lover
an' me ! *(Flinging open her dressing-gown to
show her nightdress)* Near nakedness, an' us
isn't ashamed ! No, never while love has word
to whisper, or arm strong enough t' fondle. *(To*
DRISHOGUE*)* Take me in your arms to my room
again, an' show him I am lost for ever !

> [FEELIM *appears at the opposite side of the
> room. He is half-dressed — trousers, shirt,
> and boots unlaced, with his tin hat on his
> head. He carries a torch which sends a
> stream of light over the couple. He is
> angry, and looks a little scared.*

FEELIM

Put out that light ! Turn off that switch ! Don't

you know it's not near off blackout time yet?
D'ye want th' special police-pathrols to come
prancin' in on us, or wha'? An' th' house
thremblin' over us an' undher us, an' all! What
are th' two o' yous doin'? What has yous
ramblin' round th' house at this hour for, eh?
Nice conduct goin' on, an' th' Germans only nine
waves away from th' shore! I suppose you know
there's no Tuatha de Danaan magic round here
to raise a mist, either, to hide th' shore from th'
enemy? Or raise a terrible storm, either, so's to
send their ships an' barges scattherin' to th' icy
seas in th' north, or the icier oceans to th' far
south? Can't yous see for yourselves th' way
we're tearin' down the road-signs, whippin' off
the destination names from bus, thram, an'
perambulator? Surely, it's a warnin' for sensible
behaviour to see the military goin' mad at shovin'
up concrete pillars at every turnin', and — and
hewin' deep declivities outa every road to check
th' tanks that'll soon be thundherin' down on top
of us! (*To* ABRAHAM PENRHYN) An', Farmer
Penrhyn, why are you found in the middle of
mahogany an' cushions, instead of bein' in the
centre of a field, or an orchard, tendin' growin'
corn or ripenin' apples?

ABRAHAM

Why don't 'ee keep your son fr'm molestin' me
daughter?

FEELIM

Why don't 'ee keep your daughter from molestin'
me son?

ABRAHAM

*(taking a pint bottle of whiskey from inner
pocket of coat)*

See that ? An enemy of man. Us'll make friend
of she, an' spite ye all ! (*He takes out cork, and
drinks deep.*) That's only th' beginnin'. Us'll
drink till us goes out of th' way with it, and is
ready to perish ; us'll drink till ragin' comes,
an' come in an' go out howlin', an' fair disgrace
ye all !

FEELIM

A lot of it, maybe, 'ill make you a little reasonable.

ABRAHAM

Ye is all bent in fear, an' adread of th' poppin' of
bombs. T' hell with ye all ! Hear that ? It's only
th' beginnin'. Maybe, now, you'll keep your son
away fr'm me daughter.

FEELIM

I'll do that same when you keep your daughter
away from me son.

[ABRAHAM *goes to the window, climbs over the
sill, and looks at them again.*

DRISHOGUE

Why don't the pair of you raise your voice, and
cry out halt to life ?

ABRAHAM

(warningly)

Mind ye, I'll be worse, ay, far worse, when ye

91

see me again ! (*He goes down ladder, and dis-appears.*)

> [*Outside, in the distance, is heard the faint tramp of the Home Guard, and the orders of their leader, more clear than the tramp of the feet,* " R-i-g-h-t wheel ! Left right, left right ; left . . . left.*"*

FEELIM

There — listen to that, yous ! Isn't it a wondher yous wouldn't take pattern by those gallant men, trainin', trainin', trainin' themselves to fight against the things to come ! (*He suddenly wheels right round.*) What's that ! I thought I heard a shadowy step, an' the swish of a satin flounce against me instep ! Oh, isn't it enough to have to contend with corporal enemies, without havin' to deal with spiritual ones too ! (*To the couple*) Are you sure yous didn't hear anything ?

DRISHOGUE

We've heard a lot from you.

FEELIM

(*angry again*)

You're goin' to hear more. You might have some regard for me predicamented attention to the crowd of betther people surgin' round Dame Hatherleigh tryin', through her, to touch American bankers, ambassadors, an' consuls, in an effort to get their children an' relatives quick to the States; with military critics urgin' them on with maps showin' we'll soon see the coal-scuttle helmets comin' over the hills, an' hear the jack-boots poundin' th' roads to the town's centre, to hang their hats in our own hall a moment afther. (*An electric bell gives a loud peal outside.*) There's another, now, hot-foot after a berth in a ship for America !

> [SPECIAL CONSTABLE DILLERY *appears in the doorway, flashing a huge torch over the couple and then over* FEELIM. *He is long and lanky, pale-faced and melancholy-looking, with a drooping grey moustache. He is dressed in ordinary civilian attire, covered with a fawn mackintosh, but wears a prodigiously big, hard, round-topped, thrust-out peaked cap, with a gigantic silver badge coruscating in front of it.*

DILLERY
(*flashing his torch on* FEELIM)

What d'ye mean in havin' that unobscured light there flashing about, an' th' blackout down ? Have you no thought of th' dreadful danger you may bring on people ?

> [CONSTABLE SILLERY'S *head is thrust through the open window, preceded by a big hand holding a lighted torch many times larger than that held by* FEELIM. *He is dressed like* DILLERY, *and the same huge hat, with the protruding peak, almost hides a fat, red, excitable face.*

SILLERY

(*angrily — flashing his torch on* FEELIM)

'Oo's 'ee's showin' an exposed light before black-out's over ?

FEELIM

(*impatiently — putting his torch out*)

Aw, don't go rousin' th' neighbourhood about a pin-point of light !

[*Voice of Home Guard leader away in the distance :* " Left right, left right, left right."

DILLERY

(*indignantly*)

Pin-point was it ?   It was visible half a mile down the road.

SILLERY

An' mile or more acomin' downhill.

DILLERY

Th' gleam of it dazzled me eyes moment I stepped outside of house.   Farmer Dodge said she was a searchlight gone wrong.

SILLERY

(*portentously*)

She'll 'ave t' be taken seriously, if she happens again.

[DAME HATHERLEIGH *sweeps in energetically around the piano on the left, carrying a large torch that flings a purplish-silver beam of light over the room.   Her night attire is almost completely covered with a*

94

*warm, dark-green dressing-gown, and her
feet are in slippers of the same hue.*

DAME HATHERLEIGH

What is all this ? Sillery, Dillery, what are you
doing here, instead of being on patrol ? (*Before
they can answer.*) Monica, dear, what are you
doing ? You should be asleep after being up so
late last night. The whole place is flooded with
light, the curtain is down, and the blackout time
not yet ended. Constables, you surprise me who
should be a good example to others. Did any of
you feel the house shake ? Did you hear me
asking you a question, Dillery — what has you
here ?

DILLERY

Us seen an exposed light astream fr'm window,
an' came t' investigate.

SILLERY

Us seen a bright light awaverin' over country,
an', in duty bound so to do, investigated, an'
traced it 'ere.

DAME HATHERLEIGH

Nonsense ! I hope you two men haven't stayed
too long in the Three Pigeons. Will you extin-
guish those torches at once ! You should be a
good example to everyone else, and here you both
are flooding the place with light that can be seen
miles away.

DILLERY
(*putting out torch*)

As proper authorities, we seen naked light away
off, and, after conference, traced she 'ere.

DAME HATHERLEIGH

That won't do, Dillery. When I came in, you
both had your torches flaming big as beacons.
But we'll say no more this time. But this is no
time for careless conduct. No quondam goings-
on from this on ; we must be men, and put childish
things from us. Don't you two agree ?

CONSTABLES
(*together*)

'Ess indeed, ma'am.

DAME HATHERLEIGH

Of course you do, as sensible men. It was sense-
less to floodlight the place, but inexperience
explains it all. We'll let you two constables off
this time. It'll never do to bring quiet houses into
chaos by banging on doors and ringing of bells.
Mark every circumstance well, and ponder it,
before you decide to act. Don't you agree ?

CONSTABLES
(*together*)

'Ess indeed, ma'am.

DAME HATHERLEIGH

Of course you do. Don't go painting terrors all

over the place to frighten people out of their commonplace composure. If you are frightened at anything yourselves, hide it, as brave men wearing the King's uniform, for it may in the end be nothing. No brave soldier lets his gun off at a shadow. Follow what I say, constables?

CONSTABLES
(*together*)

Us follows you, ma'am, quick an' right.

DAME HATHERLEIGH

Well, off you go home, now. (*She makes the V sign by raising the first two fingers of her right hand. The two constables, followed by* FEELIM, *do the same.*) Victory! (*She goes over to the window — to* SILLERY.) Now, Sillery, mind how you go down that ladder with your game leg! I don't want your wife to come complaining that I shoved you into needless danger. Step at a time, now.

SILLERY
(*disappearing*)

Never fear, ma'am. (*Popping head over sill again.*) No use bein' afraid — us may, like as not, be all dead soon.   [*He goes.*

DAME HATHERLEIGH
(*to* DILLERY)

A merry thought to leave with us! Eveleen doing well in the A.T.S.?

DILLERY
(*with pride*)

Lass's corporal now.

DAME HATHERLEIGH

Fancy that, now ! Tell her I'm delighted to hear
it. Off you go ; and give a hand when you can at
the digging of the trench.

DILLERY
(*as he goes out, making the V sign again*)

I will that ! Thank you, ma'am, f'r your kind-
ness. Mornin' all. Goodbye. Cheerio all.

[*He goes.*

DAME HATHERLEIGH
(*half to herself*)

Dear me, how far away some seem to be from the
discipline and dignity of the lost Ten Tribes !
(*To* MONICA) Monica, dear, go up and dress, for
now we have all so much to do that some of us will
surely end our little day before the half of it be
done. Give Drishogue a swift kiss, and be off.

DRISHOGUE
(*kissing* MONICA)

Seven days of leave left yet, Monica, so we'll be
often together, and closer than ever before.

MONICA

And may time be weary of speed at last, creep
ahead like a snail, and halt for a long rest at every
passing hour !

[*She goes, and* DAME HATHERLEIGH *comes over to place a hand affectionately on* DRISHOGUE'*s shoulder.*

DAME HATHERLEIGH

Now, my lad, who is my boy's friend, don't stay lively too long at a time, even for your love's sake. You need all the rest you can snatch away from what is still to do. Our lives no longer now are free enough to call our own. Each life is owned by all.

DRISHOGUE
(*jauntily*)

Never fear : Edgar and I'll do all things needful. We'll whizz through the sky, and turn every pouncing enemy plane into a vanishing wisp of smoke.

DAME HATHERLEIGH

I know you will do your bit, and God be wi' you both. (*She goes to turn away, hesitates, and turns to face him again.*) But listen, Drishogue, dear, and don't laugh at me or him : I cabled forty dollars over to Saskatoon's bishop for a symbol guaranteeing instant admission to heaven to the bearer, should he fall in the fight ; and a subsidiary guarantee bringing the bearer safely home. Please don't smile, if he mentions it to you, for my son is very dear to me.

DRISHOGUE

No, no, Dame Hatherleigh, I shan't make fun of it, though I advise you not to press it in his

thoughts too much ; remember his life depends
on his swift and steady nerve, how quick his
muscles answer to their tensioned call ; how taut
he is to the tip of his finger when danger flies into
the sky ; and let his guns speak straight and steady
to the very heart of what he aims at. Let him do
all this, and his little symbol will never shame
him.

DAME HATHERLEIGH

Ah ! those words, dear Drishogue, are little more
than a well-mannered mockery. (*In anguish*)
Oh ! Drishogue, we are all now in the midst of
exploding death and a consuming fire, and don't
know where to turn.

FEELIM
(*vehemently*)

Don't mind that fellow, ma'am — he's alive only
when he's conthradictin' ! You done right. You
couldn't have done a wiser or a better thing,
believe you me. What does he know to allow him
to go cock-a-hoop against the faith an' belief of
th' whole fightin' world ?

DAME HATHERLEIGH
(*vehemently — almost fiercely*)

Feelim's right ! What do you know, what can
you know of things beyond the ken of man !

DRISHOGUE
(*calmly*)

Nothing, my lady. Beyond the common news of

100

the day, I know nothing, save that on sunny days the sky is blue ; that grass is green ; and that one day leaves the house of man to let another enter.

[*With a bow to* DAME HATHERLEIGH, *he goes out. Through the doorway*, MARK *and* MICHAEL *come into the room.* MARK *carries a big cylinder tin of window security paint by its wire handle, and* MICHAEL *carries rolls of strip, adhesive paper used to criss-cross glass to prevent splintering. They come close to* DAME HATHERLEIGH, *and stand one on either side of her.*

MARK
(*hurriedly*)

Listen, now, Dame Hatherleigh ; listen t' me.

MICHAEL
(*hurriedly*)

You just listen t' me, me lady ; wiser 'n better it would be.

MARK

That's 'ee's opinion — 'taint't mine.

DAME HATHERLEIGH

Now, one at a time ; you, Mark.

MARK
(*speaking rapidly*)

Us says as how it's plain as plain as how window painted over with — with — just a second — (*he raises cylinder to read the label*) — as how window painted whole with guaranteed unsplinterable gum is as it must be more endoorable than window criss-crossed with fancy thingamajigs which is all calculated t' — t' explode like, an' pierce an' penetrate bodies that happens to be plumb in the way of glassy spikes aflyin' about reckless like.

MICHAEL

'Tain't no use, Dame, us is convinced. Spread over window endoorableness is disorganised like, us says ; an' when bomb falls — (*he puffs out his cheeks, and blows out his breath explosively*) — concussion comes on window full force, an' glass goes *Bang!*

FEELIM
(*in disgust*)

Dtch dtch — we'll never get anything done this way.

MARK
(*roughly — to* MICHAEL)

'Tain't no use, yours, us knows. (*To* DÁME HATHERLEIGH) 'Ee ain't right, me lady. See th' flaw in she ?

FEELIM

There's a flaw in the hees, too !

MARK
(*holding up the rolls*)

Not in them no. Guaranteed. Look ! Printed on 'em t' show there's no deception. See ! 'Gainst any concussion, explosion, or blast, however severe ; no flaw 'ere. Stan' behind window criss-crossed with these 'ere paper strips, an' blast

fr'm thousand-ton bomb couldn't rustle hair on
un's head !

(*doubtfully*)
I don't know — I think I prefer the sandbags.

MICHAEL
(*fervently* — *to* DAME HATHERLEIGH)
Look, lady, us'll be fair. Drop thousand-ton
bomb front of window painted with she, an' I'll
abide results if someone like Mr. O'Morrigun,
there, can be got to stan' th' test.

FEELIM
(*most indignant*)
You're damn kind, you are ! Don't you be
bringin' Mr. O'Morrigun's name into it, man !
There's no reason whatever for mentionin' Mr.
O'Morrigun's name in th' matter at all. When
are you fellows goin' to realise that what's left of
our Army's been snatched out of Dunkirk, weary
an' worn an' sad, leavin' us th' way we're without
a tank, a rifle, a hand-grenade, or a hope, with the
Germans in millions pilin' into barges all long the
coasts less than twenty miles away from us ? If
you're goin' to put th' stuff on, put it on without
any further argument !

MARK
Us thinks it's about time for an Irishman livin'
here to take an odd risk f'r th' sake of all.

That risk would be a little too odd for this Irishman to take. Look, man, when bombs are droppin', if he's quick enough, and can, this Irishman dives behind a ten-foot-thick stone wall!

[MRS. WATCHIT *comes trotting in, followed by* MR. PETER CONSTANT, *who comes close to the group, while* MRS. WATCHIT *stands a little aside, nodding her head vigorously in agreement whenever* MR. CONSTANT *speaks. He is a very tall fellow, thin as a rake, with a brown moustache pointing east and west, and a V-shaped beard, whose pointed end faces due south. He is dressed in blue shirt, green tie, grey coat, and yellow trousers, but most of these are hidden by a long, heavy overcoat reaching almost to his heels. He carries a bunch of green moss in his hand.*

MRS. WATCHIT
(*to Home Guards*)

Mind th' way, there. (*To* DAME HATHERLEIGH) Mr. Constant, ma'am ; poor man wants to get his wife away to America, an' can't ; he's all awry with the knowledge of them Germans comin' to tear 'im limb fr'm limb.

CONSTANT
(*to* DAME HATHERLEIGH)

I want you to help me to get my wife out of England. You must act quick. I've done all except get a guarantee that an American friend will take charge of her. I know none there. Please cable for this guarantee. Our income would allow both of us to live there quite well ; but this stupid Government won't let us take more than a miserable amount out of the country. I can lodge enough with you to assure your friend that he or she will suffer no financial loss.

MRS. WATCHIT
(*pitiful*)

Poor man — 'ee is in a way !

DAME HATHERLEIGH
(*coldly*)

I'm afraid I can't help you, Mr. Constant. She and you will just do what we all have to do — stay put, and do all we can to save our country.

MRS. WATCHIT
(*nervous*)

We're all aquivery with what's happened, for us knows now what t' expect when a raid comes again.

CONSTANT
(*to* DAME HATHERLEIGH)

My case is quite, quite different. As soon as the raids began, my wife became certain that she was going to have a baby.

DAME HATHERLEIGH

We'll all just have to stick it. There's no escape.

CONSTANT
(*hysterically*)

There must be ! I should be going too. I am a Liberal, and I wrote several letters to *The Times*. They'll know this, and if I'm still here, it means torture and the concentration camp for me !

DAME HATHERLEIGH

That is why we must resist. If we don't, it will mean these things for us all.

CONSTANT
(*hysterically*)

But my wife's having a baby — don't you realise that ?

FEELIM
(*impatiently*)

Man alive, that's a common occurrence round here ! That's a side issue, man. We have to use our time to prepare for the possibility of anythin' happenin'. Worse things than the raids that have already passed us.

MRS. WATCHIT

God defend we ! Mrs. Splender of the Black Diamond told 'usband that in last raid blast come in on door, ran upstairs, caught she in bath, whipped 'er un bath outa window, un set she down in middle of street. Ashamed of 'er life, she was, 'usband says, un refused to budge till Fire Brigade brought blanket. 'Usband says she says she'll never forgive them Germans.

[*A car accelerating is heard outside.*

MRS. WATCHIT

What's that, what's that ? Is it a plane ?

CONSTANT

(*squealing at her*)

Can't you hear, damn you ! You'll have us all as
jumpy as yourself. (*Shouting*) It's a car, woman !

MARK

(*to* CONSTANT)

Easy, easy, there, mate. No need to go panicky.

CONSTANT

(*savagely*)

What th' hell does she want to go all whimpering
and shaking for when she hears a car !

MICHAEL

Her heart's not shakin'. If all does as she done,
ashiverin', bombs fallin' near 'n far, amakin' tea
for us as needed it, us'll do well enough.

[CONSTABLE SILLERY *comes in, spick and span
in his uniform, with the George Medal
sparkling on his breast. It can be seen now
that he walks with a slight limp.*

SILLERY

(*importantly*)

There's a goodish crowd outside clamourin' about
th' shelters promised. Us tried to persuade them
to disperse, an' couldn't, so us selected a man of
them to come along f'r proper interrogation. (*He
calls*) Come on in, Jack !

*[A short, stout, sturdy man comes in, roughly
dressed, with a tweed cap in his hand. He
is embarrassed, but carries it off with a
defiant manner. He is followed by a trickle
from the crowd, who group themselves by
the door.*

MAN

We wants to know when shelters is acomin'. We
works hard; an' durin' nights we want to feel our
wives an' children is somewhat safe. We can get
no proper information nowhere; so we come t' see
Head Warden, Mr. O'Morrigun. (*He coughs, and
waits for comment. After a silence, he resumes.*)
People's gettin' restless, y'know. (*In a burst of
anger*) D'ye think we're made o' steel? Damn
your eyes, give us shelters!

CROWD
(*round door — chanting*)
Oh! give us shelters deep and lonely,
Where we can hide our screaming children,
To save them from the peril of living,
And from the bomb's exploding terror.

Our little homes are flaming sadly,
Death's staring in through every window;
Each thoroughfare is cover'd thickly
With twisted things that once were lov'd ones.

MAN

Coventry has got it; London has got it, and is
gettin' it still. Th' East End's smokin' rubble.

Thousands of houses are down, an' nothin' but th' poor back doors stay standin'. Th' buildin's left with their backs to th' sky are shakin'. Th' people are fightin' to live on in a forest o' fire. We've had a taste of it; but a fuller shower's bound to come our way yet. Blast your eyes, give us shelters!

CROWD
(*chanting*)

Oh, give us shelters deep and lonely,
Where we can sit in darkness quietly,
With warm arms round cold, frightened
   children,
Till evil things are banish'd utterly!

FEELIM
(*rising to his feet*)

We'll do all we can. We've done what we could, as the medal on Sillery's breast shows.

MRS. WATCHIT
(*enthusiastically*)

Ay, an' th' George Cross won be Farmer Penrhyn f'r pickin' lives fr'm blazin' buildin's!

MARK
(*slightly jealous*)

'Ee was in drink when 'ee done she.

FEELIM

Just as well he was: few men in their sober senses could have done what he did. (*Argu-*

mentatively) People, listen : Two things we have
to do — fight the raids and fight invasion. Fight
it on the beaches, among the meadows, in the
streets.

MICHAEL
(*angrily*)
How fight ? Where be th' rifles ? Where be anything ? With Bren-guns hosin' bullets on us,
bombs separatin' us, tanks cannonadin' us, us'll
have no chance ! Die in th' last ditch ? Us'll die
in th' first one jumped into !

CHORUS
(*outside the door*)
Give us th' shelters, give us th' shelters !

DAME HATHERLEIGH
Friends, we can't fight if we live all the time in
shelters.
[DILLERY, *pushing crowd aside, rushes in
excitedly, his fingers of right hand raised
in the V victory sign.*

DILLERY
(*wild with excitement*)
They've come ; at last they've come, fr'm
America — arms, arms, arms !

REST
(*together*)
Arms, arms, arms !

Tanks, planes, an' big guns f'r th' Army, an'
Bren-guns, grenades, machine-guns, an' rifles f'r
th' Home Guard !

Listen, boys ; don't get excited ; listen ! (*Excitedly he jumps on to a chair.*) Get them windows
done so's you can do some serious work — learnin'
th' stirrup-pump ; how to handle incendiaries ;
dig threnches ; camouflagin' yourselves ; an' how
to crawl, jump, run to cover of stone, three, or
bush ; how to cut telephone wires, an' how to
signal with flag, light, hand, and foot. We've all
got to stay put, an' more than stayin' put, everyone
sthrong enough to bend a blade of grass's got
to get goin', do his bit. We've got to keep th'
Jerries out ; an' if they manage to get in, we've
got to keep them fully occupied. Forward ! (*His
eloquence breaks into song :*)

> To arms, to arms, to arms !
> To arms, your ranks advance !
> March on, march on, serfdom is past,
> Set free th' world at last !

(*He jumps down.*) Come on, me lads an' lasses !
> [*He rushes through the crowd, and leads them
> out, cheering.*
>
> DAME HATHERLEIGH *stands listening to the
> cheering for a few moments, then* MRS.
> WATCHIT *comes in, carrying a telegram
> which she gives to the* DAME.

Telegram for you, me lady. Boy waitin'.

> [*As* DAME HATHERLEIGH *tears open the envelope and reads the telegram, the crowd break from the cheering into the singing again.*

CROWD
(*outside — singing*)
To arms, your ranks advance !
Give death a passing glance !
March on, march on, serfdom is past,
Set free th' world at last !

DAME HATHERLEIGH

Tell the boy there is no answer, Watchit ; and tell Mr. O'Morrigun I want him at once.

> [DAME HATHERLEIGH *sits slowly down in a chair.* MRS. WATCHIT *goes out, and after a few moments* FEELIM *comes into the room.*

FEELIM

Anything wrong, me lady ? Aren't you feeling well ?

DAME HATHERLEIGH

Get me a drink, Feelim, please. (FEELIM *hurries to the bureau, fills some whiskey into a glass, adds a little water from a carafe, gives it to the* DAME, *and she drinks it slowly.*) Thanks. A woman I know well, Feelim, has just heard that her dear husband lies dead at the front.

A God's pity that, ma'am; but I wouldn't
worry, me lady. We've too many things to
think of ourselves now without bothering about
the trouble an' sorrow of others. (*After a short
silence.*) Hundreds are in th' same plight, and
soon that black band of mournin' will circle the
arms of thousands.

DAME HATHERLEIGH

It's hard for her who has had to suffer it.

FEELIM

'Course 'tis; but we have to try to remember
that life's comin' into th' world as fast as it's
goin' out of it.

[DRISHOGUE *comes in with an arm around*
MONICA. *He is in uniform, and has his
equipment strapped on him. He appears to
be elated, while* MONICA *looks very unhappy.*

DAME HATHERLEIGH
(*surprised*)

Drishogue! Where are you going with your
harness on your back?

DRISHOGUE
(*taken somewhat aback*)

Didn't Edgar tell you that we got sudden orders
to return to squadron, and are about to say
goodbye?

DAME HATHERLEIGH
(*hurt*)

No. (*Quickly*) Couldn't find me, probably.
Where is Edgar ?

DRISHOGUE
(*jauntily*)
Bidding farewell to his lady-love, as I am.

DAME HATHERLEIGH

I see. (*Impulsively clasping* DRISHOGUE'*s hand in
both of hers*.) Goodbye, my dear boy, and God
be with you both !

FEELIM
(*piously*)
Amen ! (*To* DRISHOGUE — *trying to say it coldly*)
Well, goodbye for th' present, Drishogue.

DRISHOGUE
Goodbye, Dad.

DAME HATHERLEIGH
(*to* FEELIM)
Let's give them the last moment to themselves.
    [DAME HATHERLEIGH *and* FEELIM *go out*

MONICA
Oh ! Drishogue, God and myself only know
how much I'll miss you !

DRISHOGUE
Cheer up, darling ! It won't be long till the
golden net of reunion again entangles us in each
other's arms.

However far from Monica Drishogue may be, her love will stretch to where he is, and added length of thought will weave caresses and a prayer around him.

DRISHOGUE

However far from Drishogue Monica may be, her slim body shall feel the pressure of his arms, and her lips the warmth of his kindling kisses.

MONICA

And when he comes again, the bells shall ring his name alone; the birds shall sing his bravery; and Monica shall lead him to where all that she has shall be his.

DRISHOGUE

And a kiss shall be the song the world is singing.

MONICA

A kiss like this ! (*She kisses him.*)

DRISHOGUE

Oh ! my love, a lover's kiss is an eternal thought!

MONICA

Here they're coming.

DRISHOGUE

Goodbye !

MONICA

Goodbye ! A beggarly word braving it out to parting lovers like sorrow in a coloured coat.

[EDGAR, *garbed like* DRISHOGUE, *comes in with*
JENNIE, *followed by* DAME HATHERLEIGH,
FEELIM, MRS. WATCHIT, *and the others. The*
Purple Light appears again. The cloth
panel in the wireless cabinet shows the
swastika.

EDGAR
(*cheerily*)

Come, it's kind for all of you to gather to say
goodbye to England's newest flyers.

JENNIE

When I see you again, let the breast of your Air
Force blue glitter with stars like the sky of a
winter's night !

[*The trumpets sound the first line of " Deutsch-*
land über Alles" louder than ever, and a
clear, threatening voice proclaims, " Ger-
many calling, Germany calling," *immedi-*
ately followed by the wail of the air-raid
warning.

CROWD
(*to the airmen*)

Goodbye, goodbye !

[*The two young flyers go out. The rush of the*
German warplanes is heard in the rushing
swing of the music of " The Ride of the
Valkyries " coming close, and then fading
into the distance, as several tongues of flame
shoot up into the sky seen through the
windows. The crowd, led by MARK, *chant*

116

encouragement to the flyers and to them-
selves.

MARK
(*chanting*)

Young, lusty lads in Air Force blue,
Go forth wearing red rose and rue ;
Our life, our dreams, depend on you,
Sons of England !

CROWD
(*chanting*)

The mothers, wives, and children here,
Are nursing thoughts that death is near ;
Show them the way to cast out fear,
Shield of England !

MARK
(*chanting*)

When German proud planes zoom on high,
Teach them in th' tormented sky,
Who come to kill, remain to die,
Sword of England !

CROWD
(*chanting*)

Time shall be dead, and England, too,
Ere we forget red rose and rue,
So bravely, blithely worn by you,
Sons of England !

[" *The Ride of the Valkyries* " *swings into its*
loudest sound as FEELIM, *in steel hat and*
equipment, accompanied by the Home Guard,

MONICA, JENNIE, JOY, *and the rest stream out to do all they can to modify the destruction and uproar in the bombarded town and district, leaving* DAME HATHERLEIGH *alone gazing steadily towards the window at the rising tongues of crimson and yellow flames.*

END OF ACT II

ACT III

The SCENE *is the same, but the aspect of the big
room has changed with the changing world
outside it. Its broad and pleasing panelling
has become like the ties, the belts, and bars
connecting various parts of machinery together, and making of them an active, unified
whole. The capacious fireplace, resembling it
before, has now assumed the almost similar —
though something stylised — shape of a great
drop-hammer. The columns flanking the
doorway have become machinery shafts. The
bureau has become a lathe, though still pre-
serving the vague outlines of what it once was.
The two lesser windows have turned into
wheels carrying belts to the chandeliers, now
turned up on their sides, and ready to revolve,
too, in unison with the rest of the machinery.
Though the great room still has the shape
of its old existence, everything in it is
touched strongly with the form of its first
existence. The wireless cabinet at the back,
between the windows, is still the same. In
a corner is a rack on which half a dozen
rifles, the same number of steel hats, and
various pieces of equipment hang. Beside
them, a stirrup-pump and several long-
handled shovels for dealing with incendiary
bombs. Near the cabinet, someone is lying*

covered by a blanket ; and on the other side a form is lying, hidden in a rug. Outside tongues of flame are intermittently leaping up and down, and they can be seen through the window at the back. The black silhouette of a crane's jib passes through the red flame as if destruction and construction were battling each other. Before the central window, some dozen or so sandbags are piled in an effort to strengthen the wall under it. DAME HATHER-LEIGH *is standing rigid before them, staring out of the window, as if she had never moved from it. Occasionally a deep spasmodic shudder passes through her body, then, with a quiver, her body becomes rigid once more. Through a good part of the scene, men in over-alls and dungarees, blue and brown, cross the room, left to right, and right to left. At a table, near the jutting piano, to the left,* FEELIM *is sitting, writing out some report or other, and, now and again, giving anxious glances at* DAME HATHERLEIGH. MARK *comes in, grimy-faced, and with his uniform dusty, and the tin hat on the back of his head. He carries a long-handled shovel which he puts among the others. He looks at the* DAME, *nods meaningly to* FEELIM, *who shakes his head, and looks again at the* DAME. *As he is depositing his shovel with the others,* ERNEST POBJOY *slinks rather than walks in, carrying a basket of newly-dug potatoes on his arm. He is thirty years of age, well-made, slim, and intelligent in a curious aloof way. He can do a lot of things with his hands, is clever at vegetable culture, and has read a little. He is dark-haired, and brushes it back straight from his forehead. He can be alert when he likes, but usually goes about with his head down, and moves as if he were offering an apology for being alive. He is dressed in khaki shorts, blue shirt, grey coat, and sandals. He hesitates when he comes in, glancing at* FEELIM, *at the* DAME, *and at* MARK. *Then he slinks over to where* FEELIM *is sitting.*

POBJOY
(*to* FEELIM)
What am I to do with these spuds, please ?

FEELIM
(*curtly*)
Don't know.

POBJOY
(*slinking over to the* DAME)
What am I to do with these spuds, ma'am, please ?   [*She takes no notice.*

POBJOY
(*slinking over to* MARK)
Can you tell me where I'm expected to leave these spuds ?

MARK
(*roughly and fiercely*)
Go to hell !

[*After some slight hesitation*, POBJOY *goes slinking out by the door. The cloth panel on the wireless cabinet is lighted to show a V sign, while some mean musical notes corresponding to the letters of B.B.C., which notes are repeated three times. Then a voice calls out:* "When the siren goes, take shelter. Keep away from windows. When bombs fall, lie down." *Then the panel becomes dark once more.*

FEELIM
(*scornfully towards the wireless set*)

An' when you can't keep awake, go asleep! 'J'ever hear such nonsense! (*To* MARK) Any more news?

MARK

Didn' come on any more yet. New shift adiggin'.

FEELIM

Hear how many were brought down?

MARK

Story goes there were near to twenty o' th' bastards perished.

FEELIM
(*delighted*)

It's mountin', it's mountin'! How many of ours missin'?

MARK
(*with an apprehensive glance at the* DAME)

Dunno right; some say three; some say more'n that. God! Us is tired!

Get some sleep, boy. Watchit'll give you a sandwich ; can't get tea — no water, no gas, no nothin', be God ! Heard anythin' of Jennie ?

MARK
(*almost falling with sleep*)

No, never a word.

FEELIM

Get some sleep, boy. (MARK *goes sleepily out. After a pause* — *to* DAME HATHERLEIGH) If I were you, I wouldn't get into th' habit of standin' in front of windows, ma'am. (*She takes no notice.* FEELIM *speaks louder.*) I shouldn't get into th' habit of standin' in front of windows !

DAME HATHERLEIGH
(*turning slowly and rigidly round*)

I must watch the sky. Were I away, he might call, and I shouldn't hear. (*She turns slowly and rigidly to face the window again.*)

FEELIM

Y'know, you got no sleep last night, or th' night before. It won't do. He'll be all right. Somethin's tellin' me that. Besides, Drishogue'll keep an eye on him.

DAME HATHERLEIGH
(*musingly* — *in a toneless even voice*)

When twilight falls, the dancers come. Everywhere I go, there they dance before me.

FEELIM

(a little frightened at the mention of the shadows)
You'd no right to come out th' other night — the
bomb that fell near you gave you the shock into
imagining things.

DAME HATHERLEIGH

When Edgar goes, what's left but a poor, tired,
daft soul, who, losing her way to the door of
death, is seeking a decent way back to it. *(Suddenly)* Who are those, there, below, running
round like ants?

FEELIM
(coming to the window)
Them, me lady? Oh, them are the workmen
repairing the new factory attached to the house
here.

DAME HATHERLEIGH
(puzzled)
House here? Not here: this house can never
change; never change. *Per ardua ad astra.* A
hard high climb to the stars! *(A swift momentary
flash of flame flickers by the window. She
screams.)* The flame! I saw my son's face,
agonising, carried by in the midst of it!

FEELIM
(catching her arm firmly)
Nonsense, Dame Hatherleigh! Thry to be calm.
Thry to centre your mind on Tee-aa an' th' lost
Ten Thribes.

DAME HATHERLEIGH

(*flinging his hand off with a sudden vigour*)

Get away from me! You damned Irish! Why didn't your selfish people come over to help us!

[*The form under the rug stirs, flings the covering half aside, sits up, and shows the crinkled face of an old woman of seventy.*

OLD WOMAN

(*angrily*)

Good God! What kind of a rest centre's this! Amn't I to be let get even a minute's sleep? What's she squealin' about? Christ God! is she the one an' only one whose remembered things are the things to forget? Why don't you shut the old bitch up somewhere so's poor people can get a little peace?

[*She sinks down again under the rug, and* FEELIM *goes over to the other figure lying beneath the blanket, and gently shakes it.*

FEELIM

(*gently*)

Monica dear; Monica, darlin', wake up, will you? I dunno what to do with the Dame.

[MONICA, *who is fully dressed, slowly sits up from under the blanket, and opens her eyes sleepily.*

MONICA

What is it? More dressings and more wounds? Oh, why did you wake me, man!

I dunno what to do with the old Dame. She's
restless an' obstinate ; I thought you might get
her to keep quiet. I've a hundred reports to make
out, an' a thousand forms to fill, an' I got only a
few hours' sleep meself.

> [MONICA *reluctantly rises, and goes over*
> *sleepily to the* DAME. *A sturdy young fore-*
> *man comes in, dressed in brown overalls,*
> *with an open rule in his hand. He stands*
> *to watch* MONICA *and the* DAME. *He speaks*
> *with an Irish accent.*

MONICA
(sleepily, but with decision)

Now, Dame Hatherleigh, this won't do. You
must think of others by keeping quiet. Come.

DAME HATHERLEIGH

I don't feel able to stir. I saw something odd a
minute ago, but I can't remember what it was.
Oh ! my poor head's gone cold as if a frosty
blast had entered it by the ears.

MONICA

We'll get you a warm drink somehow, and then
you must lie down. Come.

> [MONICA *leads the* DAME *slowly out*

FOREMAN
(to FEELIM*)*

What's wrong with the old Dame ?

FEELIM

Blast shock. Doctor says time and quietness'll bring her to herself again.

FOREMAN

Two things hard to come by, me friend.

FEELIM

Did you happen to hear who were the two flyers that fell to death on th' aerodrome?

FOREMAN

They were unrecognisable. They're searching for identity discs among the pile of German burnt-out planes around them. All they found so far is a little image of an angel with outspread wings on th' body of one of them — musta been a Catholic.

FEELIM

Good God! (*Looking round to make sure* DAME HATHERLEIGH *has gone.*) Hatherleigh wore on his breast a blessed image of an angel with outspread wings!

FOREMAN

The third one, they say was some fool of a Land Girl who plunged into th' flames to thry to tear one of them free.

FEELIM

(*lifting his eyes towards the ceiling — fervently*)
From the hurt of th' burnin', from the lost alliance of loved ones here on earth, from th' blackened dust of a vanished life, give the vision of perpetual

light in th' peace of eternal rest, O God of th'
many kindnesses, and th' darin' deeds of mercy!

[*As* FEELIM *is speaking the cloth panel on the
wireless set lights up, and muted trumpets
sound the first lines of " Deutschland
über Alles ", darkening again when*
FEELIM *has finished his appeal.*

FOREMAN
(*uneasy*)

I wouldn't be dwellin' on them things! I was as
near death meself th' other night as I ever want
to be. Let's forget it. (*Indicating the blanket
and woman under the rug.*) You'll have to get
these away, y'know! Can't have th' place turned
into a slap-dash dormitory; so go to it, boy!

FEELIM
(*indignantly*)

Who're you talkin' to? Go to it yourself, boy;
or see the Welfare Officer about it. It's not my
job.

FOREMAN
(*sharply*)

Everything's everybody's job these days; so see
the place cleared, and don't argue about it.

FEELIM
(*a little incoherent with indignation*)

Who th' hell are you to give orders? We're no
way inclined to reverence fellows fresh from th'
bog; so keep your devalerian authoritarianism
quiet till you know your way betther about!

FOREMAN
(indignant now)

You shut up about De Valera. There's damn few
like him anywhere.

FEELIM

Don't I know that well — leadin' th' country to
ruin an' revolution ! Turnin' th' poor people into
shock brigades of confraternities an' holy sight-
seein' sodalities, so that they're numb with
kneelin', an' hoarse with th' dint of recitin' litany
an' prayer !

FOREMAN
(ready to go)

He done one good thing, anyway. He kept us all
outa th' war !

[*He goes.* FEELIM *goes back to the table, and
sits down. After a moment or two,* JOY,
*with other Land Girls, Wrens, A.T.S.,
farm workers, and* MARK *come in, half
pulling* POBJOY *in with them, followed by*
MRS. WATCHIT *who stations herself at the
side of* FEELIM. *The Land Girls come up to
the table ;* POBJOY *stands, hesitant, nearer
the doorway. His features are now faintly
defined as of a face appearing in vacancy.
Any old lines of determination he may have
had have lost their vigour ; and the face
has congealed into a dogged and dead con-
viction ; faint lines are there still, but
fading into insignificance, like tarnished
spangles lying in a dustbin.*

JOY

(*to* FEELIM)

Eh, you, what d'ye think us girls are ?

FEELIM

(*gallantly*)

If I told yous what I think yous are, it's not diggin' th' land yous would be, but sportin' about in the whitest o' linen an' gayest of silks, with young an' handsome gallants festooned with ordhers, an' swords danglin' from their hips, cravin' a dance in a lighted hall, or a long kiss outside, under a tree, an' the twilight fallin' !

JOY

(*in no way displeased at* FEELIM's *praise*)

None of your blarney, now ! We've come to tell you to take Pobjoy out of the fields, or we down tools ; for we won't work with a damned Conchie.

FELICITY

If he comes near where us girls work, we'll pull a limb outa him !

FEELIM

An' where is he to go ?

JOY

(*violently*)

To hell, where all his likes are stuffed !

FEELIM

Now, now ; no bad language, girls ! We'll have

to thry to look at this in a sensible way. If you refuse to work with him, he'll be a nuisance ; if you suffer him to work, he'll be, at least, a help.

FELICITY

A hindrance, you mean. *It's against my conscience*, he says, *to do anything that would lead, even indirectly, to the killing of another*. (*Violently — over to* POBJOY) If y'ever come within reach of my arm, you vacant worm, born be sleight o' hand instead of woman, I'll give your napper the weight of whatever tool I'm handlin' !

FEELIM

Now, now, Felicity, darlin', be more moderate. (*Over to* POBJOY) Come over nearer, man, an' let's have a dacent look at you. (POBJOY *comes nearer.*) See all the trouble you're causin' ? What are we to do with you ?

POBJOY

I've been ordered to work on the land.

FEELIM

Well, you see they refuse to work with you ?

POBJOY

That's your problem. I won't waste time thinking of it.

FEELIM

That's grand ! I shouldn't, if I were you. But seriously, thry to be reasonable. (*With a wink.*) Your heart's weak, isn't it, an' you were rejected

for military service ? That makes it easier for
everyone.

POBJOY

Heart's all right. I don't want to make it easier
for myself or for anyone ; besides, I don't tell lies.

FEELIM

No ? (*Exasperated.*) Why don't you say your
head is weak, then, an' clear your conscience ?

POBJOY

I gave my reasons to the court.

FEELIM

An' what did the court say ?

POBJOY

Said I was a skunk. I don't mind : I'm used to it.

FEELIM

(*wonderingly*)

I daresay a man can get used to anything in time.
Had it been said to me, I'd have cleared the
court !

POBJOY

I don't believe in violence.

FEELIM

Neither do I ; but life is full of violence, and we're
in the middle of life. Birth is noisy, and death
isn't quite a quiet thing. (*Getting eloquent.*)
There's violence in fire, wind, and water ; in th'
blast that brings a well to being ; in the plough

that cleaves th' ground ; there is violence even in th' push that sends the leaves fluttering to the ground in the autumn ; man alive, there's violence in th' struggle that gets me early up in th' morning !

POBJOY

Things you mention are natural, subsentient things — I have a conscience.

MRS. WATCHIT
(*impatiently*)

Waste o' time talkin' teh 'ee. Smack in th' jaw is grace o' God teh folks like 'im, 'usband says.

FEELIM
(*to* MRS. WATCHIT)

Wait a minute. (*To* MARK, *who bends down to whisper something*) Wait a minute, wait a minute, can't you ! (*To* POBJOY) Haven't you got any-thing in your country you admire, love, and would defend ? Surely, if they were bein' attacked, you'd defend your old churches ; the graves in which your great men and women lie ; the places where they lived ; your folk-song and your music ?

POBJOY
(*scornfully*)

No, thanks. I've no wish to dash round with the smoothing iron.

FEELIM

Come now, you do honour Stratford-on-Avon, an' the fella who wrote *Paradise Lost* ?

MRS. WATCHIT
(*ecstatically*)

Us 'eard tell of 'im — wunnerful !

FEELIM
(*to* POBJOY)

Where's this he was born ?

MRS. WATCHIT

Ah ! where indeed ?

POBJOY

I don't know — you tell us, knowall.

FEELIM

Ay, will I ; he was born in Bread Street, London, if you want to know.   Well, where was he buried ?

POBJOY

The Abbey, I suppose ; I don't know.

MRS. WATCHIT

'Ee don't know, an' 'ee don't care.   'Ee only guessed about th' Abbey.   Knowin' 'is own land's people's no importance.

FEELIM
(*importantly*)

Milton wasn't buried in th' Abbey ; he lies in th' churchyard of St. Giles, Cripplegate — where th' bombs are fallin' now.

POBJOY
(*sarcastically*)

That's hot news !

1ST FARM WORKER
(muttering angrily)

We don't want no foreigners to come 'ere tellin'
us things.

FEELIM
(ignoring the interruption)

And Nelson — come now, the greatest sailor,
maybe, that ever lived : what about him, eh ?
He's an inspiration to Englishmen, isn't he ?
(He stands up to sing :)

> Too well the gallant hero fought for England,
>   home, an' beauty.
> He cried, as 'midst th' fire he ran,
> *Nelson confides that every man this day will do*
>   *his duty !*

Come, you take pride in Nelson ; and remember
his courage an' glory to give you resolution an' —
an' fortitude in th' day o' testin', don't you ?

POBJOY

Let them who take the sword perish by it — that
is their funeral.

FEELIM

Thousands of children who never took the sword
perished by it ; perished by it because we took it
into our hands a little late.

POBJOY
(sourly)

If you want to joke, go back to your Ireland
where they like it.

FEELIM
(stormily)

Is there no fight in you at all! D'ye never feel like killin' someone?

POBJOY

No; do you?

FEELIM

I feel like it now, man! You take your rations damn quick, don't you? Yet you let brave men risk their lives to bring them here to you and your like.

POBJOY
(coldly)

They're riskin' their lives, too, for you and your crowd in Ireland, though you and they stay snug at home, safe and cheerful. Those brave men are blown to bits while your Irish eyes are smiling. Get your own rats to go into the fight, and then you'll have a surer right to lecture us.

OLD WOMAN
(suddenly flinging her rug half-way off her, and sitting bolt upright)

Ay, an' if he doesn't like us, it's easy to go to where he came from! Oh! I heard him, with his Stratford-on-Avon, Stoke-on-Trent, an' Bognor Regis. But he's too comfortable here, makin' a nice livin' outa th' soft-hearted English.

FEELIM
(to the old woman)

I was asked here, me girl: I was solicited to come here, an' give a hand with things.

FELICITY
(*fiercely*)

An' you come quick ! Yous are beginnin' to miss English rule, an' are flockin' here to oust us of ourn rights !

OLD WOMAN

As for me, no-one's prouder than me of the North-eastern Irish, who are men, an' not rattle-snakes or scum, for they belong to a different race altogether.

FEELIM
(*sarcastically*)

Didja not know that before, me girl ? We Irish are only human : The North-eastern boyos are specially adapted for divine purposes.

OLD WOMAN
(*furiously*)

North-east Ireland will remain where it is, in spite of your venom, ignorance, an' audacious intolerance. That's why your tribe never gets anywhere. After all, th' whole world knows we English are th' supreme examples of unity an' orderliness ! I hope to see all foreigners sent back to where yous came from ; an', regardin' yourself, I wish you a bomb-strewn passage over your Irish sea !

> [*While the argument has been going on,* POBJOY *has been edging back through the crowd towards the door ; and, later on, he slips away, unnoticed by the disputants.*

Us's gettin' tired of th' yarn about th' Irish as a fightin' race — if they are, where are they in this war — tell me that ?

FEELIM
(*afire with racial pride*)
Where are they, is it ?   If you were only near enough to th' centre of the flame an' th' fighting, you'd know where they were !   Thousands of us left our bones to bleach in th' Vale of Tamar, th' time Harold tried to prevent th' Norman pennon from becomin' England's banner.   Th' leopards on your banner would have jumped from th' flag had not the Irish held firm on the flank of the King's army at Crécy.   Ay, an' when your gay an' godly King Harry th' Fifth got ringed round with horsemen an' spears at Agincourt, an' surrendered himself into God's care, he didn't forget to put th' Irish in th' front of the field.

OLD WOMAN
(*mocking*)
Oh ! that time's too far off to be brought in front of us now.

MARK
(*bending down close to* FEELIM *to say in a loud, hoarse whisper*)
What are they to do with them hens us was tellin' you about ?

FEELIM
(*stormily*)
What hens, what hens ?

138

Y'know, them hens th' Food Officer wants th'
children of school teh bring 'ome on holidays,
because she can't allocate rations f'r 'em while
owners iss absent ?

FEELIM

Can't you see, man, I'm engaged on an important
discussion ?   Let th' damned hens wait a minute !
Tell th' Food Officer th' girls'll bring th' hens
home in their handbags !

FEELIM
(*to the crowd*)

We'll bring things a bit nearer.   We were at
Waterloo ; we were frozen to th' ground in th'
bastions of Sebastopol ; we were fightin' for yous
in Egypt while our mothers an' fathers were
gettin' evicted outa their poor hovels be th' land-
lords, as th' song of " Th' Irish Dragoon " shows.
(*He stands up to sing :*)

An' th' tears rolled down his sun-burned
    cheeks,
An' dhropped on th' letther in his hand ;
Is it thrue ?   Too thrue ;
More throuble in me native land !

MARK
(*in an insistent, loud, and hoarse whisper*)
What iss us teh tell officer about hens ?

FEELIM
(*ignoring him*)
An' not only yous, but others revelled in our

139

courage an' skill. Did any of you ever hear of
the Pennsylvanian Line ? (*After a short silence
— shouting*) D'ye hear me ? Did yous ever hear
tell of th' Pennsylvanian Line ?

[*A short silence.*

FEELIM

None of yous, no ! Well, they were th' best regi-
ments in Washington's Army, an' almost all of
them were Irish !

OLD WOMAN

Ay, so you say.

JOY
(*scornfully*)

Ah ! for God's sake !

FEELIM
(*rising, and advancing towards them so that
they back a little away from him*)

Ah, for God's sake, yourself ! An' we climbed
th' heights of Gettysburg, with sprigs of green in
our caps : an' thousands of us terraced the slopes
with our bodies that lie there quiet to this very day.

[ABE PENRHYN *rushes in, somewhat wild and
dishevelled. He pushes through the crowd
till he is directly facing* FEELIM.

ABE
(*violently*)

They're yeh are, asittin' in state, an' full of
audacity in doin' a neebor harm ! But God's ever
thinkin' of how best to punish ill deeds, all an'

140

sundry. Nawthin's 'id fr'm 'Ee. Where were your pumpers when farm was afire, eh ?

What pumpers ?

Stirrup-pumpers, fool ! An' y'ur fire guards an' shovellers ?

They were thryin' to be in ten places at once ; and five of them are dead.

So'm I ; near. What's left now of what stood proud, an' full of good things, with a throng o' work, makin' day pass quick, but a sulky heap o' ashes, an' coils of vicious smoke, stingin' honest men's eyes out o' them ! O God, uns all too hard to bear proper an' fit into what's meet teh say about Thy werks an' ways teh man !

Aw, poor man. A good, honest, reasonable Christian soul ! An example to all of Christian cherity en defiance.

(*slumping down on a chair*)
All is ashes an' all is dust. Us's a broken man.

Aw, th' poor man. Jeopardy 'as done for 'im !

FEELIM
(to ABE)
Get a gun in your hand an' you'll feel betther.

OLD WOMAN
Good an' proper advice. A gun's no hindrance
to a neighbourly feelin'.

MRS. WATCHIT
Ay, a sturdy un steady gun's good thing teh have
about house.

ABE
(vehemently)
No, never ! Never took life — not even rabbit's.
Us always got th' men about farm teh kill th'
rabbits. (*Violently*) Ah, God, You're too hard
on them as loves You more, an' serves You
better'n far 'an others !

FEELIM
(indignantly)
I'll not let you insult God ! Say what you like
about Feelim O'Morrigun ; but you must show
ordinary respect to God Almighty !

ABE
(rising to his feet)
I'll show ye ! Us'll spite ye all ! I've somethin'
hid away ; but us'll bring she into light o' day !

FEELIM
(earnestly)
Take my advice an' leave th' dhrink alone.

142

(*interested — going over to* ABE)

Ay, do ; bring it out, son. When a person feels
low, a drop of stimulant has a tremendous way o'
workin' good to soul an' body. Come on, son,
an' we'll get it together. (*She half leads out* ABE
around the piano.)

[*As they go out, the telephone on the table
rings a call.* FEELIM *puts the receiver to
his ear.*

FEELIM

Eh ? What is it, what is it ? Your husband must
be given another billet ? Why ? Can't get any
sleep at night because of th' fleas ? Well, what
d'ye want me to do — organise a hunting ex-
hibition ? Well, I can't help it if he does get a
breakdown because of th' fleas. Complain to th'
Billeting Officer. Oh ! you have ? Said there
were worse things in th' world than little fleas ?
I can't help it if they're eatin' him alive ! (*Impatiently*) Look here, I'm right in th' middle of an
important conference, an' can't talk, now ; ring
me up later on. (*He rings off, and gives his
attention again to the crowd.*) Listen, yous. Yous
didn't know all I'm after tellin' yous. And, if
yous even did, aself, yous wouldn't believe it, for
you have your doubts that there are stars in the
sky. Who discovered quarternions ? Who was
th' Father of Chemisthry ? (*He is nearly roaring
by this time.*) There's nothin' that we didn't
do, for in our time we were ministers, governors,
an' chancererlors. Everywhere, without skippin'

a single counthry of any known size, with a Christian thrace, or without one! But yous have forgotten your own greatness. What about your saints, with your Ha! St. George, instead of Ha! St. Edward? Where, today, is your St. Peter of York, St. Wilfrid of Ripon, St. John o' Beverley? Forgotten as well as gone!

> [*Tired and breathless, he staggers to the chair, and sits down, panting.*

MRS. WATCHIT

I wouldn't excite meself, if us was you, Mr. O'Morrigun; for it's a strain, 'usband says, as over-estimates th' system.

FEELIM

(*leaping to his feet again in a final outburst*)
An' we're here still, pierced be every bullet, scorched be every bomb, shook be every shell; an' here I am with death as close as life to me, an' a son waitin' to gamble his life in the skies for England's sake! (*He sinks into the chair again.*)

> [*The old woman comes rushing back alone, a look of wild fright on her face. She plunges through the astonished crowd.*

OLD WOMAN

(*as she rushes in*)
Make a passage there! He's on me tail! Holy God, keep th' thing quiet for a little longer!

Clear a way there ! (*She rushes out by big door-way.*)

FEELIM

(*in wonderment*)

What th' hell's happened now ?

[ABE *comes in, staggering a little. He carries a winged bomb in his arms. When the crowd see what he has, they press back to the walls. Some put chairs in front of them ; others crouch behind the table.*

ABE

(*jubilantly*)

Us found she nestin' on window-sill. (*Jeering*) Why do ye all look so anxious ? Fair surprise for ye, varmints all !

MARK

What th' hell did 'ee meddle with bombs for ? Us knows Government warned all not to touch unfamiliar objects.

FEELIM

(*appealing to* MARK)

Don't excite him, Mark.

ABE

Bombs ain't no unfamiliar objects now. Couldn't leave she sizzlin' on window-sill, could I ?

FEELIM

(*soothingly*)

There's a good man, now ; Abe, oul' son, take it away. Give it to a policeman, or hand it over to the Home Guard.

145

MARK
(*angrily*)
Us isn't trained to handle them things !

FEELIM
He must give it to someone ; it can't be left on the mantelpiece.

> [*The* DAME *comes in slowly. She is covered
> with a long black robe ; the one bright thing
> about her is a silver cap. Her face is mask-
> like in its lines of resignation. No colour,
> and little life is in her voice.*

DAME HATHERLEIGH
What is this I hear you have, Abe ? You must carry it to where it can do no harm. The house must change ; but it must not die. (*She lays a hand on* ABE's *arm.*) Each of us is very near the other now. Your home is gone ; mine is going.

ABE
(*fiercely*)
Us's a wicked daughter, ma'am, and she's brought a double woe on us.

DAME HATHERLEIGH
Your daughter's a fine girl, Abe. She must look before her ; we can only look behind. (*To* FEELIM) Feelim, guard well and cherish dearly all that may be coming to you. (*To* ABE) Come, my friend — we shall go together.

> [*They go out together. There is a silent pause
> of a few moments.*

146

FEELIM

(*in a whisper*)

Look outa th' window, Mark, an' see if you see them.

MARK

(*going to the window, and looking out*)

There they go, dimly ; goin' down the concrete way that was once th' garden path. All th' flowers are gone, though there be some do say their scents is still about th' place, 'n stronger than before. (*As the house trembles and the windows shake*) My God, what's that !

CROWD

(*together*)

The house is trembling and the windows shake !

FEELIM

(*leaning his head in his hands*)

Woe is bein' born somewhere. Jesus ! Whoever thought God would ever bother His head about th' English !

MARK

(*at window*)

An' here's Penrhyn's daughter, Monica, acomin' up what was once the garden path, an' now's th' concrete way ; acomin' slow, but acomin' sure.

[*The cloth panel of the wireless cabinet lights up, and shows the Union Jack and the Soviet Flag crossed, and fluttering, together, while a voice speaks from the cabinet.*

We wage a desperate war till death seizes the evil thing born from Germany's belly, and trained to destroy the world! British people, the Red Army's with us now! To work! Tanks for us and for them; planes for them and for us; guns for us and for them! To arms! To work! (*Voices heard singing :*)

> Heart of oak are our ships,
> Heart of oak are our men;
> We always are ready;
> Steady, boys, steady!
> We'll fight and we'll conquer again
> and again!

[*The panel darkens again. The young foreman comes in, and goes across the room. Outside, a distinct, but not loud, hum of moving machinery can be heard, with an occasional sharp clank of steel meeting steel.*

FOREMAN
(*briskly*)

Now, ladies and gentlemen, murmur your last farewell, and take your last look at the house of your fathers; for in a few minutes' time we link this with the other factory turning out tanks for the Red Army, and tanks for our own.

[*Away in the distance, trumpets and drums play soft, very slowly, and low the melody covering one or two verses of the lament, "Oh, Bend Low the Head". No one apparently hears, though* FEELIM *gives a slight indication of hearing the music.*

MONICA

(calling outside)

Feelim! oh, Feelim! (MONICA, *looking distraught, and a little dishevelled, comes in towards* FEELIM. *He rises, on seeing her so distressed, and she enters softly into his arms.*) Oh! Feelim, Feelim, pity me, and hold me close; for he was the other flyer who fell aflame from the sky!

FEELIM

(bravely, but a little brokenly)

I guessed it all along; I knew it, Monica. My Drishogue, my son! One was Edgar; the other was Drishogue. Who was the girl?

MONICA

Jennie. She tried to reach her lover, to hold him in her burning arms, and calmly died beside him!

FEELIM

We must be brave. My Drishogue! His father's lost him, but his mother has him by the hand. (*After a pause*) Does th' poor Dame know?

MONICA

She knows, though she seems to be dying on her feet. She insisted that as they died together, so they should be buried together, and one covering shelters the dust of lover and son and friend. They are here, and are to be buried now.

FEELIM
(*as if in a stupor*)
God knows I'll miss you, Drishogue !

MONICA
Are you listening, Feelim ? They're about to be
carried out for burial now. Dame Hatherleigh is
to stand by the window to see the last of them as
long as she can.

CROWD
(*who stand round with bent heads*)
They died for us all. God be good to them !

MARK
(*softly — to* FEELIM)
Us'll see teh th' hens — don't ee worry no more.

MONICA
(*gently shaking* FEELIM's *arm*)
Listen, Feelim ! The casket's covered with our
English flag ; and to keep his spirit calm beside
his comrades, I draped a silken strip of green
above our English colours.

FEELIM
That was real kind of you, now, Monica. Th' old
colour. Ay, a brave oul' flag. Is there e'er a war
known to man where it wasn't seen ? I'd be
obliged to any man who'd mention one. (*He
pauses.*) Age has twisted a little stiffness into me ;
but th' oul' eye is still clear, and th' oul' legs are

still sturdy. (*To the crowd*) Yous are askin' me silently what'll I do now, an' will I go back to where I come from? (*With a shout*) Give me me steel hat, one o' yous! (MARK *hands it to him, and he fixes it firmly on his head.*) Let the grey hair be hid behind it, for steel's a sensible embroidery for an ageing head today. (*Savagely*) Th' damned villains, bloodied all over with th' rent-out lives of child an' woman! They owe Feelim O'Morrigun a son; an', be Christ! old as he is, he'll help to make them pay to th' uttermost farthing in th' blood of their youngest an' their best! Let their bombs explode, an' wreck an' tear, an' tumble everything! It'll take more than they can make an' carry to punch us out of where we stand to fight them! (*He raises his hands in an eloquent gesture*) Hearts of steel, well tempered with hate, is what we are today — hearts of steel! Hearts of oak don't last; so hearts of steel we are!

CROWD

(*enthusiastically*)

Ay, all of us — hearts of steel!

FEELIM

(*more vehemently than ever*)

Ay, from now on to fight, harry, an' rend th' Germans till they're glad to go goose-steppin' into th' grave! Here on this spot, at this moment, Feelim O'Morrigun takes up th' fight where Drishogue laid it down! (*Brokenly — laying a*

151

hand on MONICA's *shoulder*) A cap-badge an' a few buttons are all that's left of my boy !

MONICA

(*nestling closer to him, and speaking as if it were a secret*)

There's more to come ; a living spark from himself that will soon be a buoyant symbol of our Drishogue who is gone !

FEELIM

(*his puritan nature asserting itself*)

Oh ! that was wrong of him ! I knew somethin' dangerous would come of the two of you bein' so often together !

MONICA

(*fiercely*)

It was right and proper of him, for I wanted a pledge of all he meant to me ; and I got it ; and I'm glad. Besides, we were married a month ago at a registry office ; but his dad and my dad were so contrairy that we didn't say anything about it.

FEELIM

(*shocked*)

Woman, woman, that isn't anythin' in th' nature of a marriage at all !

MONICA

It satisfies me. My dad won't, so you must stand by me now.

FEELIM

Ay, ay ; yes, yes ; but the gettin' o' children should be done accordin' to rule !

Us'll all stand by you ; an' th' babe shall become th' child of th' community.

The babe shall become the child of the community.

Oh ! Which is worse — th' burden of th' dead who are with us now ; or that of the living still to come !

> [*The trumpets and drums outside, just below the window, play the melody going with the first verse of the lament " Oh, Bend Low the Head ".*
>
> DAME HATHERLEIGH *moves in very slowly, and stands, facing forward, right in front of the window. The* DAME *is dressed in a long sable cloak, similar to that worn by* THE SON OF TIME, *which covers her completely, showing no sign of green ; and her head is covered by a silver cap, similar too to the one worn by Time's son. Her face is white, and set impassively like a mask. The coffin — half covered with a Union Jack, and half by a vivid strip of green silk — is borne in by Home Guards and farm workers, and crosses the room slowly to go out by the doorway on the right.* DAME HATHERLEIGH *turns round slowly to gaze rigidly out of the window. As the trumpets play the melody a second time, those in the room and outside sing the words of the lament :*

Oh ! bend low the head to this casket of clay,
Where young life lies darken'd while yet it is
    day.

Their laughter so young and so careless is o'er,
And their feet, prone to dance, shall be
    dancing no more.

No longer th' white apple-blossom is nigh,
And silent for ever the lassie's fond sigh ;

Th' lark's song is gone ; and they'll ne'er stir
    to see
A sky bravely blue o'er an autumn-bronz'd
    tree !

[Preceded by FEELIM *and* MONICA, *the crowd
    follows the coffin out ; the two Home
    Guards bringing up the rear.*

*When the music becomes faint in the distance,
    the young foreman, taking no notice of*
    DAME HATHERLEIGH *still standing rigid by
    the window, blows a whistle sharply, and the
    room becomes alive with movement — the
    belts travel, the wheels turn, and the drop-
    hammer rises and falls. The central wheel
    is yellow as the ripening corn ; the smaller
    ones red as the setting sun ; and the
    travelling-belts green as dewy grass on a fine
    spring morning. Through the window, the
    silhouette of the great crane's jib is seen,
    holding in its beak the silhouette of a tank
    that is swung by the window, down to the
    ground. The modified clank of steel touch-
    ing steel is heard, accompanied by the*

sounds indicating the busy and orderly hustle of a factory. In a few moments the room rapidly darkens, and at once lightens again into a vague twilight, showing the shadowy dancers grouped in the room, triangularly facing towards the window. DAME HATHERLEIGH, *wrapped in her sable cloak, and wearing the silver cap, stands rigid where Time's young son had previously stood beside the clock. Very faintly in the distance the melody — now near as vague as the twilight — of the lament can still be heard.*

1ST LADY DANCER
(to her companion)

Do you hear anything, Maurice? Listen! The sound of some very faint music sounding like a sad, a very sad, valse? Listen! The sound of silent steps around us! The dead — they make me shiver!

1ST GENTLEMAN DANCER

Some new souls seeking out companionship from shadows. But you and I can only yield a thought to them.

1ST LADY DANCER

Ah! how quick the place is changing. Smooth-faced memory is turning rough, and thrusts us out from places well beloved.

DAME HATHERLEIGH
(in a sad voice, beginning to grow toneless)

We must all go soon. Our end makes but a beginning for others.

155

1ST LADY DANCER

Where can we go, Maurice, oh! where can we go? This place only has the wistful look of eternal life.

1ST GENTLEMAN DANCER

Fear not, sweet lady: our hands still mingle, though they do not touch. Fear not, sweet lass, for shadows are immortal.

DAME HATHERLEIGH

Only the rottenness and ruin must die. Great things we did and said; things graceful, and things that had a charm, live on to dance before the eyes of men admiring.

2ND LADY DANCER

See St. Paul's standing sturdy out against the sky; and see, the people's heads are holding high, and swing is in their carriage.

> [*The sound of marching feet is heard: not of a squad of Home Guards, but of a mighty host.*

2ND GENTLEMAN DANCER
(sadly)

The people need our swords no longer.

1ST AND 3RD GENTLEMEN DANCERS
(sadly—echoing him)

The people need our swords no longer.

LADY DANCERS
(together)

Well-a-day! that ye had no swords to offer!

3RD GENTLEMAN DANCER

Look at the endless columns of marching men in brown ! Gracious God ! has colour gone from life !

3RD LADY DANCER

Don't look, don't look ! You frighten me with a vision of a dulled-out world !

DAME HATHERLEIGH

Is the crimson cherry brown ? The apple-blossom black ? The sky for ever grey ? No, no ! The cherry is as red as ever ; the apple-blossom rosy ; and the sky is often blue ; sweet lavender rears tops of gentle purple ; many a sturdy oak shall strut from a dying acorn ; and a maiden's lips still quiver for a kiss.

3RD GENTLEMAN DANCER

The lavender will bloom again, and oak leaves laugh at the wind in the storm.

DAME HATHERLEIGH

And every factory and every home will carve a niche for a graceful coloured candle. (*A little more wakeful.*) The scent of lavender's in every breath I draw, and the dancers are very close. Wait a moment for me, friends, for I am one of you, and will join you when I find my son.

[*She slowly sinks down to lean her body against the clock.*

1ST GENTLEMAN DANCER

The lavender shall bloom again !

(*together*)

The lavender shall bloom again !

[*They begin to dance their stiff, slow, but
graceful minuet, the music, as before,
accompanying them is slow, and somewhat
staccato, as if the player found it hard to
press down the notes. While they are
dancing, the voice of the* LAVENDER SELLER
is heard again chanting her wares.

LAVENDER SELLER
(*singing outside in the street*)

Ladies, buy my bonnie lavender,
Incense for your snowy sheetings,
Giving charm to all the ruling joys
Measur'd out in lovers' meetings !
Lavender, lavender,
Ladies, buy my bonnie laven-lavender !

CURTAIN

LAVENDER

Won't you buy my bon-nie lav - en - der, Ten-der
scent - ed ti - ny flower;— Giv-ing hon - ied gar-dens
to the bees, Fresh'ning ev - 'ry passing hour.— Lav-en-der,
lav - en - der, Won't you buy my bon-nie lav - en, lav - en - der?

When we stretch'd our-selves down in a hur-ry,—— Be-
-neath the soft shade of a tree,— Th' moon threw her man-tle of
sil-ver— O'er red head-ed John-ny and me;— Stars
twink-led a wel-come an' won-der'd— How we
far'd un-der Cyn-thi-a's shawl No girl ev-er suf-fer'd such
pleas-ure,— Since Ad-am gave Eve her first fall!—
Ho! then for young man an' maiden— Fair jewels of love fiercely a-
-glow— Who save life e-tern-al from fad-in', — An'
keep a tir'd world on th' go!—

SHY LASS

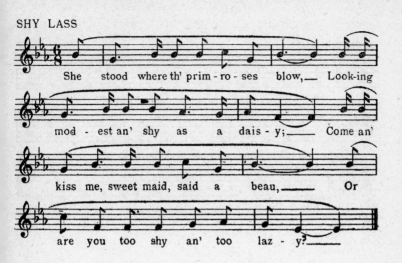

She stood where th' prim-ro-ses blow,— Look-ing mod-est an' shy as a dais-y;— Come an' kiss me, sweet maid, said a beau,— Or are you too shy an' too laz-y?—

DIGGING FOR VICTORY

Oh! here's to the trous-ers and green jer-sey too, That are out in the sun, and the rain and the dew, Un-der the sky when it's black or it's blue Dig-ging hard, dig-ging deep in the morn - ing!

GIVE US SHELTERS

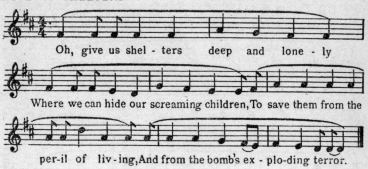

Oh, give us shel - ters deep and lone - ly

Where we can hide our screaming children, To save them from the

per-il of liv-ing, And from the bomb's ex - plo-ding terror.

LADS IN AIRFORCE BLUE

Young lust - y lads in air - force blue, Go forth

wear - ing red rose and rue; Our life, our dreams, de -

-pend__ on you,___ Sons of Eng - land!

IRISH DRAGOON'S SONG

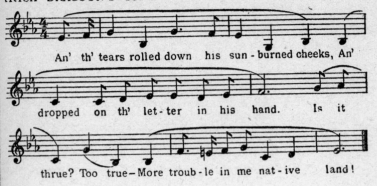

An' th' tears rolled down his sun-burned cheeks, An'
dropped on th' let-ter in his hand. Is it
thrue? Too true—More troub-le in me nat-ive land!

BEND LOW THE HEAD (Lament)

Slow and sad

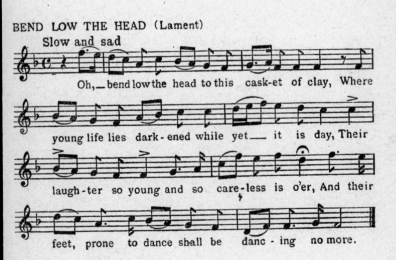

Oh,— bend low the head to this cask-et of clay, Where
young life lies dark-ened while yet— it is day, Their
laugh-ter so young and so care-less is o'er, And their
feet, prone to dance shall be danc-ing no more.

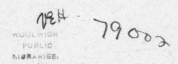

Printed in Great Britain by R. & R. CLARK, LIMITED, *Edinburgh*